The Shift

Your Journey to Overcoming Emotional Eating, Unforgiveness, and Negative Thinking

by

Karen Nurse

KNX Journey to Oneness
www.KNXone.com | knxj2one@gmail.com 440-508-6445

THE SHIFT - VIP CODE: 5573N1

AS A SPECIAL THANK YOU FOR PURCHASING *THE SHIFT*, YOU ARE INVITED TO ACCESS EXCLUSIVE VIP CONTENT FROM MY WEBSITE USING THIS CODE.

This code is exclusively for you. Please do not share it with others.

Self-Published thru KNX Journey to Oneness

To order additional copies, order through Amazon or contact:

KNX Journey to Oneness
www.KNXone.com
440-508-6445

FIRST EDITION

Book Cover Designed by Carlos Miras

Editor: Tracy Carducci

Photography:
Rodney Richards Photography
B. Vlad
Tiffany McCoy
Linda Krellner

ISBN: 978-0-578-65625-0

DISCLAIMER AND LIMIT OF LIABILITY:

The teachings, practices, activities, techniques, examples, ideas, principles, methods in this book although useful, is not to be considered as replacing the medical, psychological or mental advice of a licensed professional. KNX Journey to Oneness and the author, Karen Nurse are not providing specific qualified psychological, emotional, mental or health advice. The content in this book is to be considered as general guidelines and not as an analysis, antidote, diagnosis, prognosis, cure, recommendation or solution for specific ailments or problems. You should always consult with a qualified medical practitioner, counselor, physician or dietician before starting any health program. This book is not to be a substitute for the sound advice of a qualified professional.

Any persons dealing with anxiety, depression, stress, health or relationship issues, should consult with a counselor, medical doctor, licensed psychologist, licensed therapist or any other appropriate qualified professional. Each individual has unique circumstances and situations and each reader should take into account their specific conditions, issues and problems.

REFERENCES:

Unless otherwise noted, all biblical quotations are from the *New International Version of the Bible*.

Unless otherwise indicated, Scriptures are taken from the *Bible Gateway.* Bible Gateway, a division of The Zondervan Corporation, 3900 Sparks Drive SE, Grand Rapids, MI 49546 USA

Dear Reader,

This book is not intended to replace the expert advice that may be needed for your unique health issues.

If you have specific mental, medical or nutritional needs such as diabetes, high blood pressure, a metabolic disorder, gastrointestinal disease, a severe cardiac condition, eating disorder, depression or any other serious medical condition, it's important that you seek the advice of your own registered dietitian, licensed nutritionist, certified diabetes educator, physician, counselor or another qualified healthcare professional before making significant changes to either your diet, mental health or exercise program.

Sincerely,
Karen Nurse

Table of Contents

BOOK DEDICATIONS

Father, Son, Holy Spirit

I AM nothing without You!

BOOK DEDICATIONS (cont.)

To My Prince – My Greatest Gift

How beautiful if nothing more
Than to wait at Xavier's door
I've never been in love like this before
Now let me pray to keep you from
The perils that will surely come
See life for you my prince has just begun
And I thank you for choosing me
To come through unto life to be
A beautiful reflection of His grace
For I know that a gift so great
Is only one God could create
And I'm reminded every time I see your face
That the joy of my world is in Xavier – Lauryn Hill

My Greatest Gift. Xavier Armani Nurse, I dedicate this book to you! From the day I found out about your conception, my heart was no longer my own. You were truly created out of love. Without you I'm not sure where I'd be. You opened my heart to what true, abundant, unconditional forever love looks and feels like. You truly are my greatest gift! Thank you, Son. You gave me the freedom to express myself and encouraged me to stay committed. To be who God created me to be. I am so absolutely and utterly grateful for your love and support. For your kindness and patience. For your belief in me. For always supporting me, laughing with me, doing life with me. For walking in Jesus with me. For making my life a celebration even when it got hard. Thank you for loving, praying and even sometimes counseling me with visions, words of wisdom, and scripture all wrapped in hugs and kisses. Freedom is found in the believing in and the letting go. I love you and release you to be all that God has created you to be. Fearlessly, wonderfully, creatively, energetically, compassionately, boldly, emphatically you! Thank you for being the eyes, ears, feet and heart of Jesus. I love you with all of me!

Me: What if I fail?

God: What if you don't?

THE SHIFT - WHAT TO EXPECT

by Kara Pewthers

Karen's journey is one of massive transformation. When I first met this beautiful, strong woman I had no idea of the journey she had been on or the incredible change that she had been through. When I had the honor of reading this book, I was struck by the enormity of her "shift", and the passion she has to help bring that freedom to others.

Her story is not just about a woman's physical transformation, but of a complete "mind, body, spirit" change – and the practical ways you can have that change as well. Her weekly, step by step, approach makes these practices easy to incorporate into your life. Through personal stories and practical steps, she invites us to walk through our own transformation.

Karen's vulnerability and honesty allow us to see where she has been and validates our own struggles. But she doesn't leave us in a place of hopelessness or doubt. She walks us through ways to shift our daily actions and thoughts. This approachable book will be a guide for you as you journey towards your own "shift". Whether you are dealing with sluggishness, emotional eating, negative self-talk, or just wanting to feel better, Karen's book will help you take small actions to break out of old routines and make a positive change in your life.

Her deep spirituality and relationship with God are woven throughout her story and serves as a lifeline for her personal shift. She shares her insights and experiences with God as a way to share her internal process with us. Coming from a place of openness to the Spirit of God, Karen continues to seek health in every area - mind, body, and definitely spirit. She doesn't shy away from the powerful interconnection between these parts of our human existence. This holistic approach takes into account our thoughts, actions and experiences and helps us weave a new way of living - one that is more vibrant and healthy.

Let Karen be your guide and friend along your own transformative journey. She truly champion's the power of change and shows you how to get there - one step at a time.

FOREWORD
by Alexis Asbe

Let this be your moment.

I met Karen Nurse through a woman I barely knew. Meeting Karen did not seem significant at the time. I was in one of my drive and strive, head banging, getting stuff done, strategizing, multiplying and spread sheeting like a boss season. I was building my tribe. A powerhouse group of women that would change the world. It was a divine encounter when I heard an audible voice say, "choose her." "Choose Karen Nurse."

Challenges like raising children, heart break, drug addiction, overcoming business and health issues, long dark nights of the soul, loosing loved ones, lowest body fat ratios to highest weigh in ever, led us to prayer sessions, encouraging words, long walks and countless meetings. Karen Nurse is the moment in my experience THE SHIFT happened.

Choosing her, was choosing me. Karen has walked through the darkness, into the light and by all accounts choosing her is and continues to be a supernatural experience that has changed everything for me.

This book might be your moment. The physical manifestation, the illogical sign, the 20/20 right-of-passage that changes everything all around you. Perhaps my moment is your moment and we are all deeply connected.

My "change the world season" was futile as I was the one that needed to change. I changed by choosing Karen and this book was birthed out of one moment, one choice. This same choice may be what changes you. With infinite love for all mankind. I present to you Karen Nurse, "The Shift."

A SUMMARY OF THE JOURNEY AHEAD

Although my book, *The Shift,* very much includes stories from my life, it is not a full memoir of my life.

Yes, this is a book that will help you break free from emotional eating, unforgiveness and negative thinking; However, it does not give specific details or a chronological order of events that elaborates in depth, my journey on how or why I became an emotional eater. It's not a story specifically outlining how I changed my diet, the types of food I incorporated, my meal prep process, how long it took me to lose 90 pounds or what exercises I did to lose my stomach, tone my butt or shape my thighs. That book is to come or can be experienced through a KNX Journey to Oneness Workshop. Rather, this book outlines specific encounters where I began incorporating varying practices that created *The Shift* in my life that led me on my journey to breakthrough.

With my book, *The Shift*, I'd like to take you on your own voyage of self-discovery and impart to you the techniques The Spirit gave me that will bring healing and oneness into your own life.

Each week we will focus on one of the following techniques:

- The Art of Breathing
- Being Replenished - Water Hydration
- Fueling the Body with Life – Eating More Fruits and Vegetables
- Increasing your Physical Activity
- Meditation
- Expressing Yourself
- Asking for Forgiveness

- Speaking Words of Affirmation

- Visualization

As you embark on this journey, you will feel *The Shift* begin to take place in your spirit first, then your mind, and finally, in your body. This is not a quick fix! It's a process that requires commitment and dedication. It will take patience. It will take giving yourself grace and giving yourself the freedom to mess up, to change, and to start again, and again.

It's a journey that's going to require you to be kind and gentle with yourself, which is not easy. It's a learned practice that gets easier over time. It's a journey that encourages you to take baby steps and celebrate the small wins every step of the way. It's a journey that will be life-changing and well worth it!

As you journey through *The Shift,* you will discover your true identity, learn to love yourself, find joy in your existence, return to your God-given size, fit in those favorite jeans hanging in the back of your closet that you haven't worn in years, and use food for fuel rather than for comfort. It's **The Shift** that will empower you to believe in yourself and help you walk in your purpose.

After each chapter, you will have the option to visit my website, www.KNXone.com, to learn more about some of the techniques. For example, *Why Meditate*, the benefits of it, and an actual example of it.

Although the book, with the help of the website, is life-changing on its own, I also offer one-on-one personal coaching, group workshops, and retreats where accountability and more hands-on training takes place. You can find more information on the workshops at the back of the book.

Well enough said. It's time to get started. Are you ready to make *The Shift* in your life?

THE VISION SPOKEN

With my eyes closed, I felt *The Shift* in the room as a blanket of peace settled over me. I could sense the Divine presence more than feel it as the room became thick with glory. An inky blackness filled my eyelids as a voice that sent goose bumps up and down my arms began to fill my spirit.

"You will have workshops. Six-week workshops where women will meet together once a week to weigh in and share their struggles, their challenges, the lies they are believing."

As He spoke, I suddenly saw a dimly lit banquet room full of women of all nationalities. Some were average size while others were heavier, but most were morbidly obese. They were broken into small groups some seated on the floor, others huddled together in chairs while the rest were sprawled on the floor. Some women laid on their stomachs with their faces down weeping into the carpet. A few of the other women were crying as well while others held them close or looked deep into their eyes as they spoke words of encouragement. Others simply laid their hand on the shoulder of another as they wept with them.

I looked around the ball room fascinated by all that was taking place. Although my eyes were closed, what I was seeing was as vivid and real as if I was standing in that very space. I could feel breakthrough in the room and an excitement in me began to grow like a balloon being filled with helium.

The voice continued, *"Like Weight Watchers, you will meet weekly. The women will pray for and encourage one another. They will listen and receive a word from Me. They will journal and meditate on that word for that week, until they receive a new word when they return for their next session. You will use My Word to eradicate false beliefs with My Truth. My Word will change their thinking.*

In addition to the workshop, you will meet with these women two to three times a week to conduct a workout. As part of the program, women will have the option to attend only the workshop, or the workshop and the workouts. Lives will be changed from the inside out. As they are transformed from the inside, they will release the weight on the outside."

Then suddenly, as quickly as it appeared, the heavy-weighted presence was gone, and I could hear the music playing softly in the background and the clock on the wall ticking. I drew both hands to my chest and felt my heart beating like I had just sprinted the 100-yard dash. I breathed in deeply, smiling, content with all that I had seen and heard.

"I will name the program after my son and I, "KNX" for Karen and Xavier, but KNX will also be used as the word "connects which will focus on "Connecting the Mind, Body, and Soul through Physical Fitness, Nutrition and Emotional Healing."

My eyes suddenly snapped open as I said out loud, "Lord, people don't want to hear about you. Many people don't even believe in you. Why would a program based on your word work for people who are struggling with emotional turmoil and using food to soothe their souls?"

"Karen," I heard in my spirit, *"when people are at the end of their rope, and have tried everything they know to try and there is no one who is able to save them, what are the first words they normally say?"*

"Oh God!" I said.

INTRO - WHY THE SHIFT?

"The war against cancer has been fought with one arm behind its back and I would never go into the ring with the heavy weight champion of the world and fight with one arm," said Andrew W. Saul, Therapeutic Nutrition Specialist and author. "And yet by restricting cancer research and cancer treatment to basically drugs, surgery and radiation approaches and not consider nutrition seriously, we've done a terrible disservice to all these people."

Shaking my head, I bent over to lay my head on the desk, finding it more difficult to keep my neck from wobbling on my shoulders. The room was dark as Andrew Saul's movie, *Food Matters,* played from the projection screen in the front of the classroom. This was unlike any nutrition class I had ever taken. The food pyramid outlining the four basic food groups and daily allowances was not the subject of discussion. The room, packed with students, was breathtakingly quiet, as we hung on every word of the documentary that spoke to how a plant-based diet rich in fruits and vegetables, superfoods and high dosages of vitamins could actually reverse or even cure diseases.

I don't remember any of my mother's doctors ever using these methods as a healing remedy.

Karen, breathe, I thought, as his words were thrown at me like thick clumps of mud that splattered on my lips, eyes, throat and mouth, every word seemingly more bitter and distasteful than the last. Feeling the cold, smooth wood under my cheek, I realized they were wet with tears as Andrew Saul's next words were more incredulous then his last.

"You should do everything you possibly can and stack the deck in your favor. That means building the immune system nutritionally and using vitamins to help the body fight the disease, because being malnourished can't possibly help you beat cancer. Colon cancer" he said, causing me to jerk my head up as I inhaled sharply with the anticipation of what he would say next, "is a good place to start on because it's not very easy to treat … colon cancer is a serious disease."

"Fricking unbelievable," I whispered between clenched teeth. It was the very cancer that took my mother's life!

Saul went on, "And I would say it's a 100% preventable by having a high fiber diet and avoiding things that we know that aggravate cancer such as certain additives, foods, preservatives, environmental chemicals. They could be the cause for any number of cancers."

If only I had known. I laid my head down on the desk, squeezing my eyes shut, trying to block out the image of my mother in that coffin. "Mom, I didn't know." I was grateful for the darkness in the room, as it kept the rest of the class from seeing the display of emotions I was going through.

I tried to restrain my sobs, as I heard Saul continue,

"When we look at high dosages of Vitamin C given intravenously as an actual chemotherapeutic agent, we have wonderful uplifting news for every cancer patient in the world. And it's easy and safe, and did I say inexpensive? To have a physician give an IV, you just have to insist on it. I believe in the next 10 years this will become more accepted, but people with cancer can't afford to wait, and the ones that are already dead have been grossly mistreated by the medical profession and by the government that's supposedly supposed to encourage free research and development of all possibilities."

That was it! I felt my blood pressure shoot up like a broken fire hydrant, as my body did the same. I shoved back my chair, ran toward the door and flung it open. I couldn't take another word! I was glad I had taken a seat near the back of the classroom, ignoring the gasps and startled looks that came from the frightened students at my sudden outburst. Once outside the room, I was glad no students were gracing the hallway. The lights were off, and within several huge steps, I was in the ladies' room.

I yanked the door open and heard the bang echo loudly as it slammed against the tiled wall behind me. I was alone. Blindly, I ran into the biggest stall, no longer trying to stifle the sobs escaping my throat. Gulping for air, I threw back my head, balled up my fist, and with eyes shut, screamed with rage!

Feeling a little less pent up but now slightly light-headed, I closed my eyes and consciously focused on my breathing. As I did so, I heard Andrew Saul's words like a bullhorn, "but people with cancer can't afford to wait, and the ones that are already dead have been grossly mistreated by the medical profession". Like ice water being thrown over me, I shivered at the thought that my mother could still be alive today, if only…

"This can't be true." Looking up at the ceiling, slowly shaking my head in disbelief. "How is this possible, God? You mean something as simple as food could have saved my mother, or at the least, extended her life?"

Then I recalled … At one point, during my mother's bout with cancer, a friend of the family suggested that we try a diet she adamantly insisted changed her own life. The diet consisted of herbs, supplements and large amounts of fruits and vegetables. I could see the effects from her body, skin and nails. I relayed the information to my father, and we decided to try it. I mean, after all, what did we have to lose? The doctor's report only relayed my mother's short life span.

As my mother began to incorporate this herbal specialized program into her healing process, I noticed her health began to change. Her weight dropped over 30 pounds in a matter of months, her skin looked brighter and healthier, and she felt stronger and more vibrant. Then one day while in the shower, she lost her footing and fell. It scared us, so we decided to go back to conventional medical treatments, such as pills, chemotherapy and surgery.

As if punched in the gut by the memory, I double over, clutching my stomach at the pain of this new revelation. I now believed my mother died from chemo treatments, pills and surgeries, the very things that were supposed to save her.

Why didn't the doctors ever suggest food, diet, vitamins, and overall nutrition as a means of healing?

As I paced back and forth in the tiny stall, trying to get a grip on my emotions, I heard these words:

"My people perish due to a lack of knowledge. They don't know what they don't know until they realize they don't know it. That has been revealed to you today. Karen, you have seen people healed from debilitating diseases through My power by the laying on of hands, prayer, a command. Yes, I still do that. But if my people continue to eat and consume food as they do, without knowledge of the nutrients their body needs, how foods are processed, where it comes from or how it affects them, they will continue to consume foods that cause disease and death.

But, if my people truly begin to learn the value of plant-based foods, food created from the earth, food that is alive and filled with nutrients, vitamins and minerals, and understand the life it brings to the body, it will change lives by the millions. My people will be healed from the inside out and no longer battle these diseases that they do."

Click! It was as if I had been in a pitch-black room, someone flipped on the switch, and suddenly I could see! I felt *The Shift*! It took place in my spirit first, then my mind, my heart, and eventually, my body—

The Shift to make a change in my own health and wellness. *The Shift* to invest in research and education to learn more about a plant-based diet and the benefits of it.

I learned about the meat industry, how animals are kept in factories, shot full of hormones, slaughtered before they're fully grown, and the affects this process has on our bodies when we consume them. I learned why foods are deficient and lacking in nutrients and what foods we should consume to keep our bodies in optimal health.

I discovered the difference between "processed foods" and "living foods." What chronic diseases were, how we get them, and how they can be reversed with diet and nutrition. How doctors and pharmaceutical companies play a part, and why nutrition isn't promoted as preventative medicine or a means of healing.

As I studied, read and researched, I developed an overwhelming conviction and drive to get this message to as many people who would listen. Knowledge truly is power, and as I began to educate and invest in not only ***my body***, but ***my mind***, I began to incorporate a way of living that empowered me to take control of what I ate, how I thought, and why I made the choices I made. I believe it is now my God-given mission and purpose to help others experience *The Shift*, so they too feel empowered with knowledge to make healthier choices to live their best lives.

CHAPTER 1
LIVE AGAIN - THE ART OF BREATHING

The year I turned 50, the revelation struck me that I was on the other side of my life! Although I have much to be thankful for—a 21-year-old successful son, a thriving Transformational Coaching, Speaking and Personal Training Program, and several published stories, I haven't always been in this place.

As the age of 50 pounced upon me, I was struck by the fact that there was still so much in my life that I had yet to accomplish. It was like a hiker setting out to climb a mountain and realizing he only reached the half-way point. I had dreams, aspirations and passions that I had locked away long ago and somehow misplaced the key.

Why?

Because I was afraid. Afraid of failing, afraid of succeeding, afraid of living. I don't know. Maybe all of the above. I was living life in a Twilight Zone, an ill-defined place between two distinct conditions, nowhere and somewhere.

In 2016, while I was stuck on a carousel of emotional eating, a habit I had become very good friends with, I was standing in my kitchen on the verge of a binge when I heard in my spirit a voice that said, *"Do you think people would want you in their life if you didn't know me?"*

"Huh?" The knife I was using to smother butter on the triple decker peanut butter and jelly sandwich I was about to inhale stopped in mid-spread. My head jerked back, and I tilted my ear to the ceiling, waiting to hear more. Familiar with this voice, I asked out loud, "Wait, what?"

Then I heard, *"Karen, there's a difference between being 'hidden in Christ' and 'hiding behind Christ'"*

The grip I had on the knife loosened and I watched, as if in slow motion, its descent as it clattered to the linoleum floor. I jumped, landing with my feet wide to avoid cutting my toes as jelly splattered against the stove and cabinets.

Now, I know from experience that when God speaks to me, there's more than just His initial question. Some unpacking needs to be done. As I let the thought roll around in my head, I knew those words were just the beginning of some long talks He and I were about to have. But… not tonight. Tonight, I was stuffing those questions, my feelings and that sandwich down my throat.

Later, as I got ready for bed, feeling shame and unworthiness overtake me after indulging in yet another mindless eating binge, I caught a glimpse of myself in the full-length mirror hanging up in my bedroom. Even with the one-size-fits-all Mumu I was wearing; I couldn't hide my 200+ pound frame that protruded from under it. I stopped and stared at myself, eyes narrowing and nose scrunching in disgust. Someone had recently told me that they saw a sadness in my eyes that was there even when I smiled. Today I finally saw it for myself.

But I felt no compassion or wonderment as to why the sadness was there. Rather a feeling of self-loathing that was captured in the snarl on my face as I looked at my body. Chest, thighs and hips seemed to be everywhere as I realized I was even bigger than I was the last time I lost weight.

"Fat again!" I said softly, shaking my head and quickly turning away from the mirror, hitting the light switch on the wall as I did so. The room filled with darkness and I was relieved to no longer see that oversized image staring back at me.

How did I get here? Again!

I wondered, flopping on my bed, annoyed and frustrated. Laying on my back, facing the ceiling, I sighed loudly and raised my arms in the air. "God, what is wrong with me?" I asked, using my hands to emphasize every word. The emotion I felt caused my voice to crack. "I have dealt with this gaining weight, losing weight, gaining weight for years. Urrgh!" The growl came from deep within my throat!

"Why...do...I...keep...coming...back...here?" I waited, closing my eyes, feeling like I was bathing in loss and hopelessness.

No response.

"I feel so trapped. Like a puppy in a small cage trying to claw its way out!"

"Why can't I get out." No answer.

All I could hear was the ticking of the clock hanging from the wall.

"Are you listening to me?

"My life feels empty, purposeless. "Why am I here?"

"What am I supposed to be doing?"

Somehow the quietness made the room grow darker.

Suddenly, as if I stepped into a new compartment in my mind, a question filled my head.

When did you push the pause button on your life—when did you stop living and why?

Hmm, these were new questions. Ones I don't remember hearing before. I held my breath and waited, hoping for an answer, a word, a sign, something, anything.

"Tick! Tick! Tick!" from the clock on the wall was the only sound I heard that night and it continued as I cried myself to sleep.

Over the next few days, God began asking me questions I didn't know how to answer, like *"Who are you?"* and *'What are you afraid of?"*

When I was younger, I was full of life, free-spirited, loved to laugh, enjoyed meeting new people, traveling and taking risks. As I became a young adult, I spent countless nights in nightclubs, dancing, flirting and enjoying the attention of men. I was passionate about fitness and loved the way my body looked and responded after a daily dose of cardio and weightlifting. I made sure I wore name-brand fashions like Via Spiga, Calvin Klein, Coach, Banana Republic—clothes that enhanced and showed off my curves. I was socially available and enjoyed my life. I was unaware that my confidence stemmed from how I looked and dressed, and my identity was rooted in my size and how men saw me. Specifically, my son's father.

Our time together was like a fleeting moment. We met in a night club in Atlanta. One dance was all it took and suddenly he was moving from Atlanta to California. I was wooed and pursued with bubble baths, rose petals and candlelit dinners. His things became my things and before long we were sharing the same address.

Light, love and laughter wrapped around us like a beautiful sunny noonday. Time between us moved quickly and within a year I was pregnant.

But in my second trimester it all came to a screeching halt, ending as quickly as it had begun. Arguments, accusations and addictions moved in as well, and before long, his bags were packed, and he was checking the time as he walked out with the new shoes and watch I had just bought him.

For several months, like a stray, he was in and out of the picture. But by the time my son turned two he was gone for good and I was left to raise our son on my own.

Only I was still in what I thought was "Love."

Like a mouse in a trap, I was Stuck.

Stupid.

Sorry.

No longer laughing.

No longer living.

I held my breath, awaiting his return.

For years I asked myself what happened? What did I do? Why did he leave? But there was never an answer.

I recalled one night, after a visit from the electric company left my son and I in a blanket of blackness, sitting on the floor of my one-bedroom apartment feeling hopeless and alone. I watched the flicker from a candle and helplessly tried to console the ear-splitting cries that came from my hungry four-month-old. I bounced him gently in my arms as my own tears streamed down my face.

How do I do this, I thought, shoulders hunched. *I can't raise this little one on my own.* I felt a shiver run down my spine as the temperature in the room began to drop; I leaned back, closed my eyes, and pulled my son closer to my chest.

The thought of suicide whispered to me softly, wrapping itself around me. *It would make things so much easier.* I closed my eyes and allowed the "what if game" to begin.

The words that followed dropped somewhere past my consciousness, jolting me out of my selfishness. *"What about him?!?"* The voice I heard deep within was stern yet loving; it quickly yanked me back into the present.

Snapping my eyes open, I looked down at the little bundle I held in my arms. My son had stopped crying and was looking up at me. His eyes were wide as they searched mine. His little hand touched my cheek as if he knew my thoughts and was trying to convince me otherwise. *"What would happen to him?"* The voice continued. *"He hadn't asked to be here."*

Those questions, that truth, shook me and changed the course of my attitude, my actions and my will to live. If for nothing else, for him. At that moment, I saw my son as my greatest gift, and I felt an assurance within me that I could raise him, even if I had to do it alone. I vowed to live for my son and be the best mother I could be. My identity was now rooted in being a mom.

That night, God spoke to me, although I didn't know it was Him at the time. As I began walking with God, I started reading scriptures and learning about Jesus and the Holy Spirit. I saw that there was a difference between my internal spirit (or ego) and God's Spirit.

"For what man knows the things of a man except the spirit of the man which is in him. Even so, no one knows the things of God except the Spirit of God."
- 1st Corinthians 2:11

That night when I was alone and scared, my internal spirit was feeling overwhelmed, hopeless, and defeated so it allowed my mind to fill with thoughts of taking my life. Do you know these thoughts? Is that something you've experienced? I think we all have felt that low at one time in our lives.

But it was The Spirit of the Living God that spoke truth to me and infused me with hope and belief that I could overcome the negative thoughts I was having and bring truth to the reality of my circumstance. I was a mother to a beautiful son!

Those words changed me forever. As I raised my son, I began seeking His Spirit like hidden treasure. I knew I needed that love, peace and assurance I felt that night. So, I asked God to give me His Spirit so he'd always be with me. As I listened and followed The Spirit, I realized The Spirit was actually living in me. The love, the promises, the leading, the guiding; It was always there. He was always there. Finally, after years of pursuing me, I began to pursue Him in return.

And now, He's calling me to live again, not just for my son, or for Him, but for me.

God saved me that night and I've never been the same. I love Him. I love the relationship I have with Him. I've encountered Him in ways that I could only dream of. I love what he's done and is doing in and through me and my sons' life. He has changed my very existence and I wouldn't trade that for the world! But I believe what He's trying to show me is that the vow I made when my son was a baby is what was keeping me from living for me now that I was an adult.

Like a ceiling fan encased around a beautiful chandelier, there were two identifying factors that my life seemed to revolve around. I was a brokenhearted woman and I was left to raise my son alone. Only, now that my heart was healing and my son was a young man living his life and making his own decisions, I wasn't playing the same role in his life.

Initially, I was afraid. Afraid that he would leave me like his father. Afraid of being abandoned. Afraid he would no longer love me. After all, once he was born, I devoted my life to live for him.

However, as I saw his transition from trikes and Tonkas, to sports and girls to college and moveouts, to moving home again, I realized being his mother wasn't over, just different.

Although, the questions remained: Who was I outside of being a mom? As a woman? What roles do I play? How do I live my life as Karen?

Once I turned 50, through a series of events, something in my spirit came alive. *A Shift* took place. God began to show me I was a diamond made of fine crystal, brilliance and light. As he showed me my love and worth, I no longer felt abandoned and alone. I was no longer afraid to live the life he promised me.

The key I had hidden away so many years ago had been given back to me. Now I could unlock those jail cells I stuffed my dreams and desires in and pull them out. Feeling as free as a child on a playground, it was time to play.

As I began spending quiet time alone in this new place, I could feel myself being revived. The Spirit was breathing breath into my lungs and showing me who I was. I was digging up new treasures and exploring dreams and passions that I loved when I was a little girl. Writing is one of them. *The Shift* was happening. I was breathing again. I was being transformed.

Self-discovery is a beautiful thing. It's like a rose in bloom. You are beautiful among the vines, hidden amongst the green sepals. As you receive light, you slowly open, revealing the radiant but tiny red sprout. The deep red petals of the rose slowly break open as they embrace light, air, and water. They evolve, grow, stretch, extend, enlarge within its bud. The bright red petals unfurl across the length of its creation until it's fully in bloom, displaying all of its beauty for the world to see. Can you see yourself as the rose?

> **"Delight yourself in the LORD, and he will give**
> **you the desires of your heart."**
> *- Psalms 37:4*

Fear is no longer an option. It's time to live. To live without regrets. In order to live, you must breathe.

Will you join me?

photo credit: Rodney Richards Photography

WEEK 1 ACTIVITY:
THE ART OF BREATHING

Daily breathing exercises are very much part of the KNX Transformation Process because it's designed to bring the body into a state of deep relaxation and peace. The advantage of developing a daily breathing practice helps to regulate the heartrate, increases energy levels, detoxifies the body, improves digestion, blood flow, and sleep patterns.

This week we'll incorporate the Belly Breathing technique. Start by doing this for 2 minutes every day and try to increase by one to two minute(s) each day. Congratulations to those who have already incorporated breathing techniques into your lifestyle. You should be experiencing the benefits of this life-changing practice. For many, this will be new, so it may take time to develop the art of breathing, so be encouraged. The more you practice, the easier it will become.

Before you start your breathing exercises, under the questions below, take a mental note of how you're feeling. Are you at peace, excited, frustrated, agitated, tired, stressed? Whatever you're feeling, write it down. Then, find a quiet place where you won't be interrupted or distracted. Sit quietly and invite God's Presence into your space. Then begin to do the following breathing exercise below each day of the week.

1. Sit or lie flat in a comfortable position.

2. Put one hand on your belly just below your ribs and the other hand on your chest.

3. Take a deep breath in through your nose while you count to 4 and let your belly push your hand out. Your chest should not move. Hold your breath for a count of 4.

4. Breathe out through pursed lips for another count of 4, as if you were whistling. Feel the hand on your belly and use it to push all the air out.

5. Repeat the above breathing technique 4-8 times. Take your time with each breath.

6. Notice how you feel at the end of the exercise.

For an example of this breathing exercise go to my website, www.KNXone.com, and click the tab "The Art of Breathing" under the page labeled "The Shift."

After you've completed the exercise, reassess how you're feeling and make a note of it in your daily journal below. I've found my clients tend to hear, feel or see something in their spirit, (higher conscious, intuition or whatever you may call it) during this time. If you do, ask God to elaborate on it and write down anything you may hear, see or feel.

> **"The Spirit of God has made me, and the
> breath of the Almighty gives me life."**
> *- Job 33:4*

- Answer the three questions below.
- Pray and invite The Spirit into this moment of your life.
- Practice your breathing.

What is your emotional state of being?

_____

_____

_____

_____

What is your physical state of being?

_____

_____

_____

_____

What is your spiritual state of being?

_____

_____

_____

_____

Monday: Breathing Exercise

_____

_____

_____

_____

Tuesday: Breathing Exercise

_____

_____

_____

_____

Wednesday: Breathing Exercise (Try to increase it by a minute.)

_____

_____

_____

_____

Thursday: Breathing Exercise (Try to increase it by a minute.)

_____

_____

_____

_____

Friday: Breathing Exercise (Try to increase it by a minute.)

_____

_____

_____

_____

Saturday: Reflect on how the breathing exercise helped you this week.

_____

_____

_____

_____

Sunday: Be Still & Know –

Spend today just being still in a quiet place. In a park, on the beach, on a swing in your garden. Take time for yourself where you can be at peace. During this time, if there is anything you hear, feel, or see, write it below.

_____

_____

_____

_____

Continue to incorporate the practice of daily breathing exercises as you embark on your journey to Oneness.

CHAPTER 2
BEING REPLENISHED

Have you ever been in a place where you knew your life was about to change? Drastically? You couldn't see how, and you didn't know why, but in your gut you knew. A major *Shift* was about to take place and life would never be the same.

Picture yourself driving down a major stretch of highway; you see the road before you, miles in the distance, something visible on the horizon. Suddenly, you're rounding a bend, the brightness of the sun blinds you, and all you can do to stay on your journey is follow the few feet of road you see in front of you. A hint of fear caused by the unknown is present, but an excitement knowing you're on your way to your destination is what keeps you from coming to a screeching halt and turning around. You may slow down and begin to move forward more cautiously, but you continue to round that bend because you know where you're trying to get to is on the other side.

That's what my life felt like during this season. I couldn't see around the bend, but I was embracing the notion that life was going to be different, though I didn't know how. I felt as if I was on a roller coaster ride, being taken deeper, higher and lower all at the same time—but into what, I had no idea.

I'd have daily visions of myself in the middle of the ocean, lying face up in a rowboat, eyes on the sky, as the boat swayed to the gentle rise and fall of the waves. Water enveloped me as far as the eye could see. I looked up, legs crossed at the ankles and my hands clasped behind my head, knowing intuitively that there was a wooing within me taking place that was calling me to search deep within myself, for deeper treasure that I had not yet known or found.

I could feel the presence of peace hold me to its bosom as I looked up, the sky and ocean becoming one. There were no thoughts, no questions, no emotions, no wind or sound, just a blanket of peace that covered me. As I look back now, I would probably call it "The Calm Before the Storm."

What was God showing me as I laid on that boat with nothing surrounding me except water and sky? I'm not sure, but I knew the endless calm was inviting and reassuring. I could feel my spirit being refreshed, replenished, renewed, rejuvenated.

During this time in my life, I was 217 pounds. One of my heaviest weights. God was not only speaking to me about the importance of water mentally and spiritually for the refreshing of my soul, but also physically for the nourishment of my body. I

I was attending a nutrition class with Kele Fitzhugh at Shasta College in Redding, CA with the hope that as I re-introduced myself to the study of food for optimal health and wellness, it would transfer to my state of living. We were discussing how much water made up the human body and what the students should be consuming for our bodies to be nourished to function as it was designed to.

As I was reminded that the human body is made up of about 60% to 75% water, I realized, that my water intake was non-existent. I was consuming 2-3 cans of soda a day not to mention the glasses of juice I had with breakfast lunch and dinner. My God, my organs and joints were floating around in grape soda and Hawaiian Punch!

If I tuned into the aches and pains I was experiencing when I walked or simply got off the couch, I would have known my body was crying out for water. It was thirsty, overheated, fatigued and dehydrated. I was in a mental and physical decline.

Water serves a number of essential functions to keep us all going:

- It assists in flushing waste, mainly through urination.
- Acts as a shock absorber for brain, spinal cord, and fetus.
- Forms saliva.
- Lubricates joints.

No wonder I felt tired, irritable slow and foggy!

I learned that drinking more water also increases your physical activity performance, your oxygen levels, hydrates your cells, and causes your skin to look younger, more elastic, and moist. Count me in!

As I began increasing my water intake, I felt *The Shift* in my body. My mind no longer felt foggy, I was more energized, I slept better, and I was able to move with less pain.

To find out more information about the benefits of water and why it's crucial to the body, go to my website, www.KNXone.com, and select the tab "Water Intake" under the page labeled "The Shift."

What's your story? Are you replenishing your body with enough water? If you find that your water intake is almost nonexistent, try decreasing the amount of juice, soda or coffee you drink by exchanging one of your beverages for a glass of water.

If you're one who simply loathes the taste of water, or has a difficult time drinking it, try cutting up lemons, limes, mint, cucumbers, strawberries, oranges, or a mixture and dropping them into it. Avoid adding sugar.

So, are you ready to increase your water intake? Are you ready to experience the benefits? It's simple, practical, and highly beneficial to the overall health and wellness of our bodies, minds, as well as our emotional state. Let's get to it!

WEEK 2 ACTIVITY
REPLENISHING THE BODY – WATER INTAKE

This week our task is to focus on increasing our water intake.

Start this week by answering the three questions below. This will help you track how you feel prior to your water increase. At the end of the week, answer the same three questions again to determine if you can see a measurable difference. Give yourself a goal at the beginning of the week. For instance, if you drink 24 ounces daily, see if you can increase your intake to 32 or 48 ounces by the end of the week.

Here are some ways to gradually increase your water intake this week:

- Drink a glass of water upon rising in the morning.

- Exchange your lunch beverage for an 8 oz. glass of water with lemon.

- Choose to drink green tea instead of coffee.

- Drink a glass of water before each meal to help with hunger control.

- Exchange your dinner beverage for an 8 oz. glass of water with cucumber or mint.

- Drink an 8 oz. glass of water before having your glass of wine or cocktail.

- Drink an 8 oz. glass of water before your workout and one after your workout.

- Drink an 8 oz. glass of water a few hours before bed.

Increasing your water intake this week will cause frequent trips to the restroom, but remember, you're hydrating your body, flushing out toxins and revitalizing your skin, hair and nails. As you continue to consume water, overtime your need to use the restroom will decrease.

As you enter this week, make a note in your daily journal below of how you increased your water intake, the amount you increased it to, and how you felt after doing so. Make a note if there was any difference you were able to discern from the increase. (See Monday's example below.)

Remember to consult your doctor, dietician or family physician if you're taking any medication or on a special diet, as it may affect your daily water intake.

How are you feeling emotionally?

_____

_____

_____

_____

How are you feeling physically?

_____

_____

_____

_____

How are you feeling mentally?

_____

_____

_____

_____

Monday: (Example: Today I had green tea instead of coffee with my afternoon snack. I felt good about the exchange. I found I did use the bathroom three times today before 2:00 p.m. Normally, I use it once. I didn't feel too much of a difference.)

_____

_____

_____

_____

Tuesday:

_____

_____

_____

_____

Wednesday:

_____

_____

_____

_____

Thursday:

_____

_____

_____

_____

Friday:

_____

_____

_____

_____

Saturday:

_____

_____

_____

_____

Sunday: After this week's water intake, answer the questions below.

How are you feeling emotionally at the end of the week compared to the beginning?

_____

_____

_____

_____

How are you feeling physically at the end of the week compared to the beginning?

_____

_____

_____

_____

How are you feeling mentally at the end of the week compared to the beginning??

_____

_____

_____

_____

Can you see or feel any differences in your body, mind, emotions, sleep patterns, alertness, focus, etc. since increasing your water intake this week? Make a note of them below.

_____

_____

_____

_____

Continue to incorporate the practice of consuming 64 ounces of water daily and your daily breathing exercise as you embark on your journey to Oneness.

CHAPTER 3
FUELING THE BODY WITH LIFE

After being chained to a desk and chair for over 15 years, I started praying for *a* S*hift* in my life. I wanted more quality time with my son and the opportunity to go back to school to obtain my bachelor's degree in psychology. When I was laid off from Yahoo in December of 2010 and an opportunity to move to Redding, CA came along, I jumped at the chance! Not only was I able to begin home-schooling my son and create lasting memories with him, I could finally return to school and begin attending the world-renowned Bethel Church, where I believed I would receive great spiritual healing and teaching.

After leaving the Bay Area, it wasn't long before the new environment, missing family and friends, and trying to stay positive for my son began to wear on my spirit. Four months of rainstorms with hail as big as golf balls that kept us bound to the house didn't help. With one dully lit lamp, dreary white walls and thin windowpanes, the house never felt warm and cozy.
So, like an old friend, I turned to food as my outlet. It wasn't long before depression set in and the pounds begin to creep up my hips and thighs again. I was finding it more difficult to stay in that place of excitement I had upon moving there.

Months later, as we began adapting to our new city, the sun finally came out of hiding and Redding's heat proved to be hotter than an oven on broil. We'd simply step 20 feet from the front door to the car and find ourselves in a pool of sweat that trickled down our backs and legs. But we were happy as we began adjusting to our new environment. I enrolled my son in school and followed suit. I was thrilled to finally be inching my way towards my psychology degree.

I signed up for a nutrition class unlike your average "Eat the Four Basic Food Groups" class. This class focused on the processing, manufacturing and storage of our foods. It spoke about the life expectancy of fruits and vegetables and the difference between "living food" and "dead food."

We watched movies that exposed how animals were no longer grown on farms and fed seeds and grains. It revealed how chickens and cows were housed in factories and cages with the most immoral living conditions. It showed calves, piglets and baby chicks being injected with hormones to age them faster and increase their size to meet consumer demands.

As my "Intro – Why The Shift?" section identifies at the beginning of the book, this is NOT the story where I will go into step-by-step details about what I began to eat, the exercises I began to incorporate or the time I dedicated to it. It does not give a stroke by stroke paintbrush picture on how I changed my life and ultimately took responsibility for my health and wellness, resulting in me releasing more than 90 pounds. That book is to come. However, I wanted to expose to you some of the reasons why I began changing what I put in my body. The biggest change was the transition from eating "dead" food to "living" food.

Keeping a journal opened my eyes to how much processed or "dead" food I was filling my body with. I was consuming foods like frozen chicken strips, frozen French fries, frozen pizza. ice cream, cakes, candy and cookies in an overwhelming abundance. Boxed macaroni and cheese. Canned beans with hot dogs. And fast food like McDonald's, Carl's Junior and Burger King was also high on the list.

When I did eat wholesome meals like baked potatoes, chicken and salads, I would drown them in fatty butters, oils and salad dressing.

Where were the enzymes? No wonder I gained weight, had little energy and felt tired and drained most of the time.

The nutrition class encouraged me to gradually start adding more fruits and vegetables to my diet. Easily enough, as I implemented these new habits, I began feeling the benefits. There was *a Shift* occurring in the decisions I was making that began to take shape internally. I got fuller faster and felt more satiated, which caused me to cut down on the junk food between meals.

As I began feeling more energized and restful, I started replacing the junk foods with healthier choices. For instance, I traded my 3:00 p.m. bag of chips for an apple with almond butter.

I was able to walk and move my body more freely, the pounds began to shed, my clothes fit better, and I was feeling lighter and more mobile. The decision to make healthier choices was transformational. It was like putting a new engine in a car. The spark plugs fired up, an explosive shock charged the engine, and the motor was coming to life. *The Shift* began happening externally.

Are you ready to fire up your engines? I want to help you embark on the journey—the journey of taking your health back? We're going to start by taking baby steps toward choices that will empower you to make a lifelong permanent change. Knowledge is power! As you know better, you do better!

Are you ready to do something as simple as adding a fruit and vegetable to your meals? It's the path that helped me to lose more than 90 pounds. Honestly, how much fruits and vegetables does the average American consume? Probably not enough!

For more ideas and information on the variety of fruits and vegetables you can add to your meal as well as meal options, go to my website, www.KNXone.com, and select the tab "Clean Eating" under the page labeled "The Shift."

WEEK 3 ACTIVITY

INCREASING YOUR FRUIT & VEGETABLE INTAKE

This week we'll plan to add a fruit and vegetable with your meals. In addition, we'll ask that you keep a journal of what and when you ate which will help you track what you're consuming each day of the week. Track your food consumption for breakfast, lunch, and dinner, including any snacks. Continue to track your water intake as well.

To ensure you meet your daily intake of fruits and vegetables, try to plan out your meals and what you'll have for each meal at the beginning of the week, or at the least, the day before. Do your best to incorporate a vegetable and a fruit with each meal.

Before starting your journal, answer the three questions below.

What types of food does your diet currently consist of?

_____

_____

_____

_____

_____

How much fruits and vegetables are you currently getting in your diet?

_____

_____

_____

_____

_____

How do you feel after consuming your current diet?

_____

_____

_____

_____

_____

Monday: Keep a journal of what you ate today, ensuring that you add a serving of fruit and a vegetable with each meal, and make a note of how you feel at the end of the day. (Do this for each day of the week.)

_____

_____

_____

_____

_____

_____

Tuesday:

_____

_____

_____

_____

_____

_____

Wednesday:

_____

_____

_____

_____

_____

_____

Thursday:

_____

_____

_____

_____

_____

Friday:

_____

_____

_____

_____

_____

_____

Saturday: Reflect on how you feel at the end of the week compared to how you felt at the beginning.

_____

_____

_____

_____

_____

_____

SUNDAY: Be Still & Know –

Spend today just being still in a quiet place. In a park, on the beach, on a swing in your garden. Take time for yourself where you can be at peace. During this time, if there is anything you hear or see, write it below.

_____

_____

_____

_____

_____

_____

Continue to incorporate the practice of daily consumption of fruits and vegetables, 64 ounces of water intake and your daily breathing as you embark on your journey to Oneness.

CHAPTER 4
PHYSICAL FITNESS =
MOVING YOUR BODY

I come from a family of dancers, so ever since I was a little girl, I loved to dance. In elementary school, I would watch my brother and sisters perform in their high school talent show, and when I attended high school, I followed in their footsteps.

Enrolling in a dance class as a high school junior, I began choreographing dance moves with a group of friends. During lunch, we'd practice in the gym while half the school watched and cheered us on. It wasn't long before we began performing at school rallies, talent shows and school competitions.

My love for dancing didn't stop after high school. It evolved into physical fitness activities like Zumba, Kickboxing, Taebo, Turbo Jam and Hip-Hop dance. If I wasn't in a class, I was at a nightclub. Throughout my young adult life, I spent my nights dancing into the early hours of the morning, eager to learn the latest dances, from the Freak, to the Cabbage Patch, to the Bank Head Bounce, to the Tootsie Roll. At the end of the night when the MC shouted, "You don't gotta go home, but you gotta get the hell out of here!" I would be drenched with sweat, smelling of smoke, and grinning from ear to ear. I was disappointed that it was over already, but always excited that I'd be back again the following night.

I was often complimented on how fluid I moved to the music while adding my own spin and flare to it. I was always eager to help others learn the moves as well. So, when people began encouraging me to get certified as a dance or fitness instructor, I loved the idea and earned my first Group Fitness Certification from the YMCA. I started teaching classes at Cisco Systems in their fitness department, and like a kid who had found their favorite toy, I was hooked!

As a Group Fitness Instructor, (Aerobics Instructor is what they called us back then), I discovered I carried a power to create! As the instructor, when I walked into a studio ready to teach a class, I could command attention simply by standing in the front of the room. Eyes from the back, front, side and middle were glued to my every move, watching, waiting, and prepping in anticipation for me to take a step, lift my arm, or roll my hips, all with the intention of imitating my every move.

Many times, I didn't use words. I'd point to the left, then to the right, or simply lifted both hands, palms facing out, and the whole class would come to a standing march, like an army of soldiers. My rhythm, my style, my form of expression, demonstrated with hops, spins, twists and kicks, all tailored to an eight- or sixteen-count beat, was exhilarating as the students mirrored my every move. They plugged into me like a lamp into a wall socket, my energy fueling their own as a synergy developed that kept us collaborating in unison to every beat and motion.

After having my son, I quit my extracurricular activity of dancing at the nightclubs and took on a corporate job at Yahoo where I no longer had the bandwidth to teach fitness classes regularly. My work was demanding and the hours, long. I no longer devoted as much time to physical fitness. Late night dance sessions were traded in for long hours sitting on a rolling chair in a 6x6 cubicle. I tapped endlessly on a keyboard with my eyes glued to a computer screen, desperate to finish a report or plan an event before leaving for the night.

Corporate America taught me that the reward for a job well done was more work. And although I enjoyed my job, the only person looking after my son and my well-being was me.

It wasn't long before 10 hours days sitting at a desk, corporate meetings with fluffy mashed potatoes and gravy, rosemary chicken and rich desserts along with a lack of exercise began showing up on my body. The added stress, heightened emotions and sleep deprivation also took away from the attention, care and love my 11-year-old son needed. This sedentary lifestyle was not benefiting myself or my son.

Something had to change. I had to make *a Shift.*

I started with my job. When 4:30 p.m. rolled around, I checked out—not only physically but mentally! I closed up my computer and no longer accepted any calls from work. I realized that whatever didn't get done today, would still be waiting for me in the morning. I began spending more quality time with my son: taking walks through the park while stopping to play a game of catch. When the weather was nice, we'd take a swim in the pool, a walk along the beach or ride our bikes. Picking up a game of basketball at the local gym or going to the movies was another favorite pastime. We were moving and enjoying not only life, but each other. Physical activity was not only helping us to get in shape, decreasing my stress, but it was creating an unbreakable bond between mother and son.

What I've learned as a Health and Wellness Trainer is that the benefits of moving the body doesn't only affect your physical wellbeing, but your emotional and mental wellbeing as well. When you move your body…

1. It can make you feel happier.

2. It can help with weight loss.

3. It is good for your muscles and bones.

4. It can increase your energy levels.

5. It can reduce your risk of chronic disease.

6. It can help skin health.

7. It can help your brain health and memory.

8. It can help with relaxation and sleep quality.

9. It can reduce pain.

10. It can promote a better sex life.

This week, I'll help you focus on moving your body to get you in the best physical shape for your body, heart and mind.

To discover how much physical activity you need and how much time you should spend engaging in it for the best health benefits, go to my website, www.KNXone.com, and select "Physical Activity" under the page labeled "The Shift."

Are you ready to start moving your body in order to experience the benefits above?

WEEK 4 ACTIVITY
INCREASING YOUR PHYSICAL ACTIVITY

This week we will incorporate physical activity through movement.

As I mentioned, physical activity can improve your mind, body and emotions. This week, as you move your body, we want you to monitor your physical, mental and emotional state of existence from the beginning of the week until the end.

Start by working at your own level. Whether it be working in the garden, taking a walk, using the stairs instead of the elevator, rollerblading, jogging, swimming, jumping on the trampoline, dancing, etc.

Consult your physician before engaging in any type of physical activity if you are taking medication or have a chronic disease. In the back of this book, you will find a Pre-Screen Health and Wellness Questionnaire to complete prior to starting your exercise regime this week.

Remember, this is a journey, not a sprint. If you haven't engaged in physical activity for some time, you're in pain or struggle to stand for long periods of time, listen to your body and start gradually: 5-10 minutes on a treadmill, take a walk around the block, use the stairs instead of an elevator, or use a chair. Start by sitting in the chair and gradually increasing your heart rate by doing arm circles, arm raises, knee lifts, leg lifts, etc. For exercise ideas and workouts, check out my website at www.KNXone.com.

For some of you, this may be the first time you're engaging in physical activity in quite a while. Give yourself grace. Do what you can do, then be sure to celebrate the small wins. If it's walking around the living room three times, acknowledge that fact and congratulate yourself for doing so. Understand that the more you engage in physical activity, the stronger you become and the easier it gets.

For those of you already engaging in physical activity, excellent! Kudos to you! Try doing an activity you've never done before in order to broaden your abilities, such as Pilates, yoga, or surfing.

Start this week by answering the three questions below. Then select a physical exercise that you will do. Try to get in a workout at least three times this week.

How many days do you currently exercise? _____

How many days will you plan to exercise this week? _____

What will your exercise consist of?

_____

_____

_____

_____

_____

_____

What are some things that you can do to ensure you stay committed this week?

_____

_____

_____

_____

_____

Monday: What exercise or movement will you do today? How much time will you spend doing it? Please be sure to capture how you felt after completing your physical activity.

(Answer this question for the rest of the week).

_____

_____

_____

_____

Tuesday:

_____

_____

_____

_____

Wednesday:

_____

_____

_____

_____

Thursday:

_____

_____

_____

_____

Friday:

_____

_____

_____

_____

Saturday: Write down how you are feeling, emotionally and physically after engaging in exercise this week. How were you feeling at the beginning of the week vs. the end of the week?

_____

_____

_____

_____

SUNDAY: Be Still & Know –

Spend today just being still in a quiet place. In a park, on the beach, on a swing in your garden. Take time for yourself where you can be at peace. During this time, if there is anything you hear, feel, or see, write it below.

_____

_____

_____

_____

Continue to incorporate the practice of daily movement, eating a fruit and vegetable with every meal, drinking 64 ounces of water and doing your daily breathing as you embark on your journey to Oneness.

CHAPTER 5
"IS SEEING BELIEVING?"

A few years ago, on a warm spring evening, I was seated at the table of an elegant upscale restaurant, enticed by the streams of sunlight bouncing off the Sacramento River and the calming tranquil sounds it made as it rushed down the riverway. I sat with four beautiful women who captured not only the attention of the men at the other tables, but that of the women as well. As my eyes examined each of them, I felt like a piece of gum one of them had stepped in and I was now the unseen sticky goo. Sitting with them, I couldn't figure out why I was there. My mind was displaying a flashing orange neon sign like the kind you find on the highway that says "DETOUR," only mine was saying, "YOU DON'T BELONG HERE."

We had gathered to discuss a project they were trying to implement for a women's TV daytime talk show. They thought I would be excellent as the fifth host. As exciting as it sounded, all I could think about was how out of place I felt.

I perceived these women to be high-profile, well educated, influential business owners with money! Their salon-style hairdos, brightly colored, perfectly manicured nails, flashy rings, and expensive clothes draping their sun-tanned, toned and curvaceous frames were something I only dreamed of obtaining. Their chatter and laughter filled our little table as they reminisced over the wine and luxuries they had indulged in during a Vegas trip the weekend prior, the countertop marble one of them had purchased for a vacation home, and a trip to Hawaii one of them was surprising her children with.

I remained quiet, keeping the menu close to my face, chewing on my bottom lip, eyes darting from one entrée to the next, finally landing on the "petite salad" that was just under $8.00. I breathed a sigh of relief, mumbling to no one in particular about getting the salad because I wasn't really hungry. *Someone else would have to pick up the tip*, I thought, as I placed the menu down and gave the women another once over. I was a single mom, in between jobs with $10.00 in my purse.

What could I possibly bring to the table? I was wondering if the diners at the other tables, those sneaking peeks our way, wondered the same. As my eyes landed on each of the women at my table, I could see why the other women in the restaurant, like thieves, stole glances at them as often as the men did. I was doing the same. Catching every subtle movement. The wind blew gently, causing the skirt of one of the women's dresses to rise slightly, showing off her toned, crafted legs. Another tilted her head back and laughed, exposing the small nape of her neck and the long, gold strand earrings dangling from her earlobes. The smiles that radiated from beautifully colored lips. One leg gracefully crossing the other. The wisp of hair one gently tucked behind her ear. The way one held her pinky out while she sipped her glass of wine. All of this spoke to their femininity, their womanhood. They embraced it, no, actually *wore* it, with dignity and grace. Feeling frumpy, I crossed my legs at the ankles, my wide pant legs hiding the turned over, scuffed black flats I wore. I slumped a little lower in my seat, like a child pouting, trying to imagine what it would be like to live in their freedom.

I wished I hadn't agreed to come. Their conversation was light, fun, and filled with laughter. My own unworthy thoughts limited my participation. I felt small, intimidated, fat, black, and so out of place in the outdated black slacks and cotton wrap I wore. My nappy hair, almond skin, big lips, wide nose, thick thighs, and full hips on top of an almost 200-pound frame did not belong in this circle of successful, straight-haired, ivory-colored, thin-but-strong women I sat with.

Oh God, why did I come? I remained still, quiet, like a phone on silent; I didn't want anyone to know I was there. With my shoulders hunched, eyes down, watching my hands wring in my lap, I wished I was invisible. I felt like an ugly duckling in the midst of swans. Could they sense my unworthiness? If so, no one said anything.

The women's voices rose and fell as the discussion moved from the aspiring TV show, their professions, travel, politics, visions, expectations and dreams. Although I was dialoguing in my own head with my negative thoughts, I was immediately tuned into the conversation as it turned to the Bible and Scriptures. Knowing how much God had changed my own life, He was always a topic I couldn't help talking about. One of them turned to me and said, "Karen, do you know what scripture I'm speaking of?" All heads turned to me, eyes of wonder and anticipation meeting mine, waiting. For the first time that night, I felt seen.

With the spotlight on me, I slowly sat up in my seat, lifted my shoulders, straighten my back as a sense of pride filled me. I cleared my throat as if I was about to perform. "As a matter of fact, that can be found in *Romans, Chapter 3*." With all ears attentive and eyes on me, I proceeded to spend the rest of the evening trying to prove, with bible verses and the knowledge of God, how worthy I was to be a part of this "exclusive" women's group.

When the night came to a close, we hugged and said our goodbyes with the promise to meet again in a few weeks.

As I drove home alone, the battle in my head began again. *Those women look like models. Did you see their sculpted legs and thighs? You are so far from that,* came the first blow. Tears began to well up as I tried to defend myself, *Yes, but I've been working out. I've lost some weight.*

So what! came the second punch. *Even when you lose weight, you* always *gain it back. You lost 30 pounds last year and found 40 more this year!*

"Karen, you are wonderfully made in my image. I love you." That still small, familiar voice chimed in, giving me the courage to speak up.

It's not always about weight, I defended, wiping my tears in frustration. *Those women think I would be the perfect addition to the show. They said I could be the next Iyanla Vanzant, you know, from that show "Iyanla, Fix My Life." I could help people fix their lives.*

I pulled into my parking stall in front of my apartment and turned off the ignition. *You can't even fix your own life!* the voice snarled. *You don't have a college education; you pause midsentence, unable to find words to finish your thought and you do not speak as eloquently as they do. You would never make it as a talk show host."*

Like a dull knife, the hurtful words continued to gnaw away at me, causing me to forget the encouraging affirmation the still small voice spoke to me.

And let's not talk about those black pants you have on with the worn seam between the legs! Please! You can't afford sundresses or heels like they wore! You could barely afford the salad! And look! Your nails are jagged and with overgrown cuticles. Not even a clear coat of polish on them! My eyes moved to my hands, before quickly folding them in my lap.

When's the last time you even had a manicure? the voice said mockingly. I shrugged, wondering the same. I closed my eyes and shook my head, trying to shut up the voice. Tears ran down my face as I found myself screaming, "Enough!" Burying my head in my hands in defeat, I wept bitterly, knowing the negative voice had won again. "You're right, I don't and never will fit in!"

The following day, I spoke to my girlfriend, who had introduced me to the group, sharing with her how I felt that night. She tried to help me see what they all saw in me that I couldn't see in myself. My beauty, my kindness, love and graciousness, my intelligence, my value and worth. How God created me and what was in me. But her words fell on deaf ears. Her affirmations were not nearly as loud as the negative self-talk that played repeatedly in my head.

As I went through my journey into Oneness, God reminded me of this day and how I had felt. As you can see, my biggest obstacle was me. The thoughts I entertained in my head, and the lies I believed. For years, two of those women and so many others, tried to help me see my real identity. It took years of afternoon talks, walks, friendship and prayer before I finally began to see even a glimpse of the beauty, uniqueness and purpose that these women saw in me. I was the Daughter of a King.

So, now let me ask you, have you ever felt the way I felt that night? How many of us refuse to embark on our path to our purpose because of how small we see ourselves, the lies we believe about who we are and what we carry? Why do we find it so difficult to see past our shortcomings? Why don't we believe in our own beauty, individuality, courage, love and creativity? Why are we constantly comparing ourselves to others? How do we become bold, brave, fearless, ferocious, and comparable to no other? How do we eradicate negative thinking and false beliefs in order to walk in wholeness?

When you give yourself permission to journey through this book, and actually commit to and apply the work each week, you too will experience *The Shift!* You will see that with self-love, transformational coaching and spiritual healing you will bring your mind, body and soul into alignment and walk in the fullness of who God created you to be.

I'm happy to say, as I walk out my journey, because I believe we're always on one, my life has truly shifted. I think, see and embrace the beauty around me and within me. I love myself and feel worthy of love. Something I haven't felt since I "stopped breathing." I now live in this alignment, this oneness! Is life perfect? Absolutely not, but I can say I'm living again.

As I've learned to love and live in this new existence, I've decided that my passion, my purpose, my servanthood will be for others, for inspiring multitudes, for changing lives. But my walk, my will to live, my life will be lived for an audience of One. And in Him, I'm already approved. And so are you. Do you believe this?

My desire now is to help you walk in the same reality. I hope, as you continue to read my story and see me shine my light, it will inspire you to shine yours as well.

WEEK 5 ACTIVITY
LET'S MEDITATE

This week you will spend time meditating and asking God to show you how He sees you, taking your negative thoughts and exchanging them for His words that speak of love, life and freedom.

Although there are many definitions and ways to meditate, According to Wikipedia, "Meditation is a practice where an individual uses a technique—such as mindfulness and stillness by focusing their mind on a particular object, thought or activity—to train attention and awareness, and achieve a mentally clear and emotionally calm and stable state."

"Keep the book of the law always on your lips and meditate on it day and night, so that you may be careful to do everything written in it. Then you will be prosperous and successful."

- Joshua 1:8 NIV

- Spend five minutes practicing your breathing exercise.
- Sit facing a mirror and spend five minutes looking at yourself: Your face, eyes, neck, hair, body, etc.
- After doing so, ask yourself the three questions below. How are you feeling physically, mentally and spiritually?
- Then answer the questions for each day of the week.
    - Start with the question you ask yourself.
    - Then, with the question you are to ask God.
- Write down what you hear, feel, or see, no matter how abstract or abnormal it sounds. Spend time meditating on it. You are made in God's image, so His words will mirror who He is.

To see an example of the Mirror and Meditation Work Activity go to my website, www.KNXone.com. Select the "Meditation" tab located under the page labeled "The Shift."

How are you feeling physically in your current state?

_____

_____

_____

_____

_____

How are you feeling mentally in your current state?

_____

_____

_____

_____

How are you feeling spiritually in your current state?

_____

_____

_____

_____

Monday:

What do I see when I look at myself?

_____

_____

_____

_____

God, what do you see when you look at me?

_____

_____

_____

_____

Tuesday:

What do I love about myself?

_____

_____

_____

_____

God, what do you love about me?

_____

_____

_____

_____

Wednesday:

Why do I believe I am here? What is my purpose?

_____

_____

_____

_____

God, why am I here? What is my purpose?

_____

_____

_____

_____

Thursday:

What would life look like for me if I trusted God completely?

_____

_____

_____

God, what would life look like if I trusted you completely?

_____

_____

_____

Friday:

What would it look like to trust God with my family, my dreams, my future?

_____

_____

_____

_____

God, show me what it would look like to trust you with my family,
my dreams, my future.

_____

_____

_____

_____

Saturday: Reflection

Spend today meditating on things God has spoken to you during
the week. Write down any additional things you may see, hear, or
feel.

_____

_____

_____

_____

Sunday: Be Still - No questions today.

Spend today just being still in a quiet place. Take a bubble bath,
have a candlelit dinner on the patio, spend time in nature. Make
time for yourself where you can be at peace. If there is anything
you hear or see during this time, write it below.

_____

_____

_____

_____

Continue to incorporate the daily practice of meditation, being
physically active, eating a clean diet, drinking 64 ounces of water
and doing your breathing exercises as you embark on your journey
to Oneness.

CHAPTER 6
FINDING YOUR VOICE

Who stole my voice?

After my son's father left me to raise our son alone, I shut down my feelings and became mute. I never truly expressed all the pent-up feelings I was harboring inside, hoping that if I didn't say what I was experiencing in my heart, he would eventually come back to me. He's unfaithfulness and lies were not enough to close my heart to him although I wished it was.

I wanted to say things like, "Why did you leave? What about your son? What did I do wrong? Can I fix this? I love you. Please don't go!" to things like, "You hurt me! I don't need you! You ain't s---! I hate you!" Instead, I remained quiet and carried around my emotions like baggage.

I was hopeful that he was just going through a phase and things would change. I saw him sparingly as it was but was devastated when one day, he told me that he was moving back to the east coast to restore his relationship with his father. Imagine that! And just like that, he was gone, leaving me to raise his 16-month-old son alone.

My heart ached too much to be angry, so instead, I'd cry myself to sleep at night after spending yet another day trying to answer the oh-too-many "where is my Daddy" questions. I was holding out for hope that if he didn't come back for me, he would come back for his son. I watched, waited and prayed for years, hoping that we'd be a family one day. But we never were.

I never expressed to him fully what his leaving did to me or our son because I thought if I spoke my truth, it would quench that flicker of hope that one day, he'd return.

As the years rolled one into another, my heart eventually healed. However, I still allowed myself to be disrespected and dishonored when it came to this man. The year my son turned 15, we went to visit him and after encountering that oh-too-familiar treatment, I knew enough was enough.

I had finally become a woman who learned how to value myself. Not based on how skinny I was, how much money I had, what I wore, or the mistakes I had made. I finally knew my worth and virtue, for my Maker is my husband. He called me back after I was deserted and distressed in spirit. And my identity was no longer wrapped up in this man or what he thought of me. *The Shift.*

My identity was in God, who said I was rebuilt with jewels of turquoise, emeralds and rubies; my gates are now all sparkling jewels. My son will be taught by The Spirit and great will be his peace. No longer did I feel that my son had to have his father in his life for him to be all that God created him to be.

While God was doing this deep-seated work in me, *The Shift* happened. He showed me that no one ever "stole" my voice; I gave it away. The only way I could walk in my purpose and speak for myself or on behalf of the King was to take it back.

I started by writing the letter below. Like a shaken can of Coke, I exploded. Years of pent up hurt, anger, pain, and heartache rushed to the surface as I spilled words onto paper.

No longer would I allow myself to be held in shackles to the way this man treated me. Like a balloon, I was releasing him today. Regardless of what he thought, how he responded, or how he felt, I needed to do this. Even if I never sent the letter, I knew I had to write it. In doing so, I was actually setting myself free.

THE LETTER

For years, I traded my voice in for peace, for doing the right thing, or for simply needing to be accepted. But I'm learning that, in giving my voice away, I'm hiding behind a shell of security that is nonexistent. I'm pretending and I no longer want to. Being a Christian does not mean I have to be a doormat for others or that I cannot express myself in ways that will be freeing to me. So, I'm going to do that today.

It takes time, energy and effort, and quite frankly, being present, available and accessible to raise a child. And believe me, it wasn't always easy. I did my best to raise a boy into a man. But, where have you been the last 15 years?

God helped me to realize that my son is brilliant! And all of his boldness, energy and grandioso personality are to be for the Prince of a Man he is becoming. But nobody tells you these things, so you have to learn them through experience, through heartache, through faith, and love. The bond between mother and son grew. Where were you?

How do you soothe the soul of the one who doesn't know or understand that his father leaving him, has nothing to do with him? How do you answer the questions, "Where is Daddy? Why doesn't he call or come see me? Why doesn't my Daddy want me? Will I ever have a dad?" Well, will he?

Do you know what it feels like to love someone sacrificially? How about loving someone to the end of yourself? Where you become nothing so that they become everything? I can give him the best schools, clothes, homes, etc., but there is one thing he longs for that I cannot give him. So, I cry, and I pray that one day, YOU will turn your heart toward your son. Until you experience this kind of love, it would look abnormal to you looking in. I love hard for him. I would walk to the ends of the earth for him. I would die for him, lay down my very existence for him. Can you say the same?

Being a parent requires sacrifice, requires love beyond yourself. And it's not always easy. Knowing what to say or how to say it, how to listen, hear his heart, push past the need to always correct is difficult! How could you ever know what it feels like to love someone with such a part of you that you would put them before your own needs if you don't stick around long enough to make it happen? To endure the good, the bad and everything in between?

I no longer want to be in bondage to this hurt, anger or animosity that I've felt toward you. I also refuse to live my life based on emotions that were birthed from lies. You do not get to dictate to me my identity. You do not affirm me as a woman. How you treat me or feel about me does not determine my worth or value. What you say to me or think of me does not override what God says about me as a woman, as a mother, or as a child of God. So, I give back to you all that is yours and I take back from you all that is mine.

I renounce the lie that I'm a witch, controlling, or that I'm trying to curse you in any way. I renounce the lie that I act more like a girlfriend to my son than I do a mother, and Lord, I ask for forgiveness for partnering with these lies. I ask for forgiveness for all ungodly thoughts that I've had toward this man. And I forgive you, cover you and release you to God to be all that He has created and ordained you to be as a man, as a father, and as a child of God.

As I closed the letter, I felt *The Shift*. A heavy blanket of oppression was being lifted. Chains were being broken, and I felt like a kite being released in the wind.

WEEK 6 ACTIVITY
USING YOUR VOICE TO SET THE CAPTIVE FREE

This week's activity is a 2-part assignment focused on Setting the Captive Free–Yourself.

The first part is to either write a letter, make an audio, or record a video addressed to a person, (for instance, a parent, spouse, child, friend, girlfriend/boyfriend, sister, brother, aunt, or even a stranger, etc.) that:

1. Hurt, disappointed or took advantage of you and you've found it hard to forgive the person.

2. You're still angry, embarrassed, ashamed, or afraid to express your feelings because you don't know how they are going to respond.

3. Has passed away and you still have anger or hurt feelings toward that person but never had the chance to express them.

4. Physically or verbally abused, sexually traumatized, abandon or manipulated you and you're still feeling scared, used or victimized.

Many times, when we bottle up our emotions and fail to articulate them, it can begin to take shape in our bodies as illness, disease, obesity, depression, etc. As we release these emotions, we no longer have a need to feed them. Ultimately releasing us from those ailments.

After you write your letter, pray and see if you are supposed to send it to the person, (or burn it, bury it, rip it up, etc.) This is an act that is designed to not only set you free but set the person free as well. This activity is to help rid you of old hurts or unforgiveness and bring healing, so you no longer carry around emotional baggage.

Let's begin by engaging in your breathing exercise. Start with 2-3 minutes of breathing. Once you feel centered, invite The Spirit into your time.

After doing so, write down every feeling, thought, and emotion you want to express but haven't found the courage to say. Please do the exercise even if the person is no longer with us.

After releasing your emotions using whatever method you choose, spend time being quiet. Ask The Spirit to show you any areas where you may need to forgive yourself for partnering with or believing any lies that were said to you, or that you told yourself. Write down everything that comes to mind.

For instance, perhaps your husband made you feel like you weren't worthy of love and you began believing that. Forgive yourself for doing so.

FYI, as things are revealed to you, it may invoke a great deal of emotions. As they come up, try not to suppress them. If you need to get up, take a break, cry, go for a walk, talk to a friend, pray, etc., do so, but come back and allow the emotions to play out.

This is a purging process. Imagine you have a clogged drain. And you used a snake to unclog the immediate blockage. If not done properly, there may still be gunk, slime, hair and sludge clinging to the sides of the pipe or worse, the clog is just pushed down further in the drain resulting in a greater blockage later on. We want that blockage cleared completely. Don't you?

The second step is an activity I acquired from Lisa Nichols, the world-renowned motivational speaker, best-selling author and CEO of Motivating the Masses along with some direction from The Spirit within.

If you want to see an example of the work required for setting the captive free, go to my website, www.KNXone.com, and click on the tab 'Setting The Captive Free" under the page labeled "The Shift."

The second part of this week's activity is forgiving yourself. You will experience *The Shift* in the perception of who you are and what you are deserving of. Like climbing Kilimanjaro, reaching the top, seeing the endless sunrise, and claiming victory with a white flag, you will discover that you are worthy of forgiveness. You are worthy of love. A love worth dying for.

You will learn how to become your biggest cheerleader and your greatest encourager. Why? Because The Spirit lives in you and your past does not define who you are. Like the endless blue sky, you were created to have life and life abundantly. That life looks much different than the way you've been living it. You will begin to release those pent-up emotions you've been carrying around like a backpack.

After writing the letter, before starting each day, take time to breathe for 2-3 minutes. In your quiet time, ask God to reveal to you 5-7 things that you want to:

1. Forgive yourself for.

2. Promise to commit to yourself.

3. Celebrate yourself for.

Once you receive the answers, spend time looking at yourself in the mirror. Speak to yourself with kindness, gentleness and love, as if you were speaking to a child or a loved one. And use the three sentences below. This can be done upon arising, before you go to bed, or whenever you can make time for yourself.

After completing this exercise, in the space provided under each day of the week, write down anything that comes up for you.

We believe healing will come from this activity, so take your time. The hope is that as you do this exercise, the situations you need to forgive yourself for will decrease, giving yourself the grace and love you deserve.

_____ *I forgive myself for (write down whatever you've been holding against yourself):*

_____

_____

_____

_____ *I promise to (write down a promise of how you will love yourself going forward):*

_____

_____

_____

_____ *I celebrate myself for (write down something that you can celebrate yourself for):*

_____

_____

_____

_____

Monday:

_____

_____

_____

_____

_____

Tuesday:

_____

_____

_____

_____

_____

Wednesday:

_____

_____

_____

_____

_____

Thursday:

_____

_____

_____

_____

_____

Friday:

_____

_____

_____

_____

_____

Saturday: Reflection

Spend today meditating on things God has spoken to you about during the week. Write down anything you may see, hear, or feel.

_____

_____

_____

_____

_____

Sunday: Be Still & Know –

Spend today just being still in a quiet place. In a park, on the beach, on a swing in your garden. Take time for yourself where you can be at peace. During this time, if there is anything you hear or see, write it below.

_____

_____

_____

_____

_____

Continue to incorporate the mirror work, meditation, being physically active, eating fruits and vegetables, drinking 64 ounces of water, and doing your daily breathing as you embark on your journey to Oneness.

CHAPTER 7
"LIVING WITH THE CHOICE" - FORGIVENESS

"How many babies do you think you have in heaven?"

The still small voice asked, shooting goosebumps up my arms and causing my spirit to stand at attention. The random question was so unexpected that I stopped in my tracks, holding the lever of the frozen yogurt dispenser in one hand, an empty bowl in the other.

It was a late summer afternoon in Redding, CA and God had been speaking to me quite often lately, bringing up situations that I had forgotten about, but obviously, He hadn't. I would suddenly have a vision, thought, or question about something that happened in my past.

As three droplets of the chocolate treat fell into the empty container, I closed my eyes, briefly thinking, *Wait, what?*

"I will question you and you will answer," the voice said gently but firmly. This time slower, with more emphasis on each word, the question was asked again. *"How... many... babies... do... you... think... you... have... in... Heaven?"*

The question tightened my belly and gripped my heart with such intensity that I knew it was coming from a higher place than my own conscience. I also knew that the answer was not going to be resolved with a simple tally.

I let go of the lever and slowly stepped back from it, rolling the question around in my head; I whispered it to myself a couple times, then said, "Where is this coming from?"

The higher voice said, *"Come now, let's talk about this. Where your sin is crimson red, I will make it as white as snow."* Having lost the desire for the creamy chocolate, I sat the empty container down on the counter, walked outside of the shop, and took a seat at the metal table under the awning. *How can you ever make that sin okay?* I wondered.

The answer started with a memory.

> *The door to the waiting room opened. "Karen Nurse." The pounding of my heartbeat sounded like a drum base in my ears as a flood of questions filled my mind.*
>
> *What am I doing? Why didn't he come? Should I have made him come? What will he think? Will he leave me after this?*
>
> *Gripping the side of the chair, I could feel the numbness begin in my fingers as I stared at the nurse, wide-eyed. I was frozen with fear. Although I was 25, I felt like I was 5 again—scared and alone on my first day of kindergarten, with a sea of faces staring back at me.*
>
> *After quickly surveying the other women in the pale blue waiting room who were either filling out paperwork, flipping through magazines or simply staring out the window, the nurse's eyes finally landed on mine. I must have had a look of pure terror on my face, because she walked over to me. "Karen?" she questioned again, bending over so we were at eye level, her voice much softer as I nodded slowly.*
>
> *She put her hand on my shoulder as if to comfort me. I slowly released the edge of the chair and rose to meet her. As she led me to the rooms located on the other side of the waiting room doors, she took my arm, probably guessing that at any moment I could pass out or perhaps run. As she did, the scene from the night before began to play in my head.*
>
> *"Are you sure you want to do this?" We were seated on opposites sides of the bed, our backs facing each other, so I*

couldn't see the look on his face. I glanced over at him to see if he was serious.

"What about me?" He was bent over tying his shoes, his voice void of much emotion. "I am the father." He sat up and turned to look at me. "Do I have a say in the matter?"

I ignored the hint of emotions I saw in his eyes that his words were not relaying. This was not the first time the question had come up, and frankly, I was tired of talking about it. Did we really have to have this conversation right now? Right before work! I exhaled loudly, hoping he'd get the point. I was sick of the conversation.

"Come on!" I rolled my eyes and slammed my fists on the edge of the bed. "I have dreams and aspirations just like you!" Getting up, I moved from the bed to the dresser. Picking up an earring, I began putting it on as I continued. "Besides, we've only known each other a few months!" I faced him. "Why do you want another one anyway? What if 'we'—I paused, pointing from him to me and back to him again— "don't work out? My life stops as you run off, free to 'play house' with the next female?" He stood, staring at me as if he was seeing me for the first time.

"After all," I continued sarcastically, lowering my voice, "how do I know you won't walk out on me?"

"I wouldn't" he turned away from me, shoulders slumped in defeat as he walked into the small bathroom.

"It's my body!" I said, my voice rising as he closed the door behind him. "This decision doesn't really affect anyone else but me!"

The sun was beginning to set as I sat in front of the yogurt shop, trying to manage the emotions the memory was creating. "That was over 17 years ago, God. Why are you bringing all of this up now?" As I saw a couple approach, I quickly lowered my head and abruptly wiped away the tears, avoiding their questioning glance as they walked by.

"So, how many?" the voice asked again. The same heart-racing reaction rose again, only now with an overwhelming desire to reach out to the man who would have been the father, to ask him the same question.

Sensing this was bigger than either one of us, I sent him a text. "Hey, I have a weird question to ask."

"What is it?" he texted back immediately.

I could sense his guard go up even though I wasn't speaking to him personally.

Feeling my own defenses rise, but not enough to break communication, I tried to stall, "I'm sorry. I know you may be at work so this may not be the best time."

"Just ask!" was his crisp reply. *Oh boy*, I thought.

"This is such a random question, I know ... but, well, here it goes. How many babies do you think you have in Heaven?" I hit send and placed the phone on the table, rubbing my hands together nervously.

My phone went dead silent. His response didn't come as quickly as his previous ones, so I jumped when my phone buzzed loudly as it moved across the table almost 10 minutes later.

"Wow" was all it said. My sentiments exactly.

While I waited, the sun had dropped behind the mountain, leaving only the top to peek over it. The red and orange hues threw shadows across the parking lot. 20 minutes had passed, and my phone remained silent, leading me to believe that our conversation was over. I got up to leave the yogurt shop, the question and recollection still heavy on my heart.

As I went to bed that night, the vision of that day in the doctor's office so long ago began to play again like a video.

"Here we are." The nurse said, snapping me out of the memory of the conversation I had with the would-be father the night before. She led me into the procedure room. "Go ahead and put this on." She seemed detached, almost mechanical as she handed me a worn, faded gown. I wondered how many other girls had worn it before me.

"The doctor will be in shortly." I avoided her gaze, heart still galloping like a racehorse. "Hey," she said softly, my eyes locked on hers, as I held my breath, hoping she'd say the words that would make all of this somehow seem okay. "It won't hurt, you'll feel some pressure and small cramping, but it will be over before you know it." She gave me a reassuring smile that didn't make it to her eyes before closing the door behind her.

She was right. It was over before I knew it. And I didn't cry. Not in the doctor's office, or the recovery room, on the drive home, or even when I went to bed that night. It was a couple of weeks later that the truth and finality of what I had done hit me. I had taken a life. The life of my baby! Suddenly, like a dam breaking, every emotion imaginable—sadness, regret, anger, dread, disbelief, fear—all consumed me at once and the tears came like a flood.

Remembering that fateful day brought up emotions that I hadn't felt in years. As I rolled over onto my side, pulling my knees to my chest and thinking about what could have been, I cried myself to sleep.

The next morning, I was reminded again of the question the small voice had asked. *"How many babies do you have in heaven?"* Later,

I received the answer from the one who would have been my baby's father. His text simply said "2."

Stirred again by that higher consciousness, I closed my eyes and tuned in, *"Those two babies he speaks of, the voice said gently, with compassion, are yours as well. Before you even knew you were with child, I knit them together in your womb, set them apart, and called them mine. The rejection of my gift to you was not hindered by your choice. You see, I had already prepared a place for them so they would be here with me, where I AM."*

As I heard His words, tears began to roll down my cheeks. I had been crying often the last two days. A friend told me years ago that tears were like liquid prayers, so I had learned to embrace them. I needed prayer more than ever right now.

Emotions that lay dormant came flooding to the surface as the archives of my life flashed before me. Where guidance and wise counsel were lacking, hasty, hurtful, heartless decisions had been made, leaving me scattered and fractured.

"The answer is simple", the voice continued, *"I know you and call you to humility; seek what is right, turn from the bloodguilt."*

As a 25-year-old young woman, I couldn't see how a choice I made then would affect me so drastically at 48. My decision to have an abortion affected not only me, but my future unborn children, my son, the father who didn't have a choice, his family, my family, and the generations that followed.

Proof of this fact came when I shared my experience with my son as a teen and had to rock him in my arms as he cried, grieving at his missed opportunity to have a sibling. It's been a secret that I've carried for years, and although God has done much healing in me, I believe through this, He wanted me to see that there was still hurt and unforgiveness that I had caused, which prevented me from being fully one with The Spirit, myself and with others.

Earlier in the week, a friend of mine had invited me to gather for prayer and worship. This was normal, as I attended events like these frequently. However, as I drove to the address, I couldn't help but feel like this was somehow a set-up, although I had absolutely no plans of bringing up what I had been reminded of the last couple of days. But as I gathered with those women to pray, God knew what needed to be healed. So, I was not too surprised when my friend said hesitantly, "I don't know why, but I feel like we're supposed to pray for abortions." Never having had an abortion, I could hear the wonder in her voice as to why that thought popped in her head, but I knew.

I shared with them my own experience and what the small voice had been communicating to me. After doing so, we began to pray. Years of suppressed emotions surged through me, causing me to drop to my knees, bury my face in the plush carpet, while my eyes overflowed with tears; I wailed bitter, anguished cries that spoke of heartache, pain and shame.

As words like "Lord forgive us, we repent, have mercy, restore us" filled the room, deep, wrenching sobs shook my body as I wept for my unborn children. I wept for my son, their father, our families. I wept for other mothers who aborted babies and still felt shame, guilt, and unforgiveness. I wept for fathers who never knew or had a choice, and for babies who never had a voice.

After some time, our prayers turned to worship and declarations of purity, holiness, righteousness and restored families. I imagined thousands of babies and angels in heaven, rejoicing with laughter and praise in celebration. Silencing lies, and accusations being brought against mothers who had aborted their babies but were still living in the shadows of shame and condemnation. As they rejoiced, I felt *The*

Shift. Chains were breaking, hearts were being healed, and parents were being set free. We were being redeemed.

As I reminisce about this day, I realize that God desires us to be healthy and whole in every area of our lives, with nothing separating us from Him. This unconfessed area kept me from being fully connected. I was feeling detached and fragmented. Although the Lord had forgiven me for my selfish act, He tells us to confess our sins, one to another, and when we do, we will be made whole.

That night I lay in bed, feeling wave after wave of love wash over me, the small voice that was becoming more familiar chimed in yet again, *"Your sins are forgiven!"* I smiled, floating in an ocean of peace. *"However, knowingly or unknowingly, you have caused grief. You grieved me as well as the people you love. Go show them love as I have shown love to you. Seek forgiveness. When you confess your sin, be humble, gentle and patient, standing with one another in love. I will create in you a clean heart and renew a refreshed spirit within you. Breakthrough will arise and the message of reconciliation will come upon you, your family, and the millions you share this with."*

Like the gearshift of a car moving from idle to drive, I felt *The Shift*! A transfer of power to forgive surged deep within me. A few days later, I knew I had to call and say I was sorry to the father of our unborn child. Yes, there was fear initially. How would he respond? Would he reject me, accuse me, lash out at me? I wasn't sure, I just knew it was an act I had to carry out.

Cracking open your chest and exposing your heart for others to see leaves you open and vulnerable. There is always that fear that you won't be seen, heard, or understood when you reveal raw, naked emotions as pure as asking for forgiveness. But I did it anyway. Because, in that moment, my desire to please God was greater than my fear of man. Regardless of how he responded, I was sure that one day, even if he didn't receive it now, it would bring healing to his heart, just as it had brought healing to mine.

I finally understood that trying to hide old wounds in my heart was preventing me from receiving God's healing, power and love in these areas. With His compassion, I am clothed in compassion, kindness, humility, gentleness, and patience, which allows me to walk in freedom, helping others to do the same. When we are forgiven, we can truly forgive, and in doing so, live fully in Him, walking in our true identity as children of God.

Is there someone in your life who you need to forgive? Someone who needs to hear the words, "I'm sorry?"

WEEK 7 ACTIVITY

FORGIVENESS – SAYING I'M SORRY

First things first, let's just stop for a moment and be still.

Close your eyes. Take a deep breath by inhaling slowly from your nose as you count to four.

Now hold your breath for an additional count of four.

As you exhale, release your breath from your mouth for another count of four.

There. feel better? Are you ready to continue? If not, complete the breathing exercise a couple more times.

As I wrote this chapter, I felt a flood of emotions rising from the dead. Emotions I wasn't ready to embrace or even deal with. So, as you read this chapter, you too may find yourself face to face with some unexpected memories of your own that you have no desire to relive. And believe me, I understand.

However, those feelings, those memories those pent-up emotions were the driving factors that led me to use numbing mechanisms like food, Netflix and YouTube to escape from the feelings within. Those memories that I refused to deal with were the very ones that were causing me to isolate myself from the freedom, peace, healing and abundant living that was meant for me.

Although your story may be different from my own, whether it be a molestation, a rape, sexual or physical abuse, a divorce, a father who left you, etc., you may still experience a tsunami of emotions this week stemming from your traumatic experience.

As you begin the activity for this week, if you're feeling that this process is too overwhelming or difficult to continue, please seek professional help from a counselor, physician or mental advisor. It is okay to ask for help.

Before you begin, let's invite The Spirit into how you're feeling. What are the emotions that are coming up for you right now? Are you angry, scared, upset or feeling alone? If so, ask God to help you to deal with these emotions. Invite The Spirit to come be that comfort that you need. Some of my clients found it difficult to find peace in God because they were asking questions like *Where were you? How did you let this happen? Why didn't you protect me?*

If those questions are coming up for you, make a note of them. Then ask those questions out loud. God can handle it. After asking, wait. Wait for the peace to move forward. If you still feel anxious or upset, take a walk, say a prayer, write in your journal or talk to a friend.

Then come back. Stay engaged. Come face to face with how you're feeling. I know it's scary. I know it's uncomfortable but remember you're not alone. You have an internal advocate who's leading you through the process and desires to bring healing and wholeness to your heart, soul and mind.

As the memories or events begin to play, you may try to suppress them. In fact, you may have already made a trip to the kitchen for a bowl of ice cream or a bag of chips and don't recall doing so.

You may be feeling like you can't read another page. You may want to skip this chapter altogether or put the book down for a few days as you process. That's okay—remember it's a journey. Your journey and you're not going it alone.

Take it one day at a time and give yourself grace. Continue to do the work, stay close to The Spirit and believe that He will finish the work He started.

This week we're going to ask you to do a series of tasks. Can you humble yourself and ask for help, say I'm sorry or seek forgiveness? Even if you believe you have a right to how you feel, are you willing? I know how difficult it is to reach out to someone when you're angry, hurt, ashamed, guilty, feeling low or unworthy.

But you've been holding these feelings hostage, locking these emotions in your body and soul. When we suppress our emotions, research shows we can become mentally and physically ill, tired, emotionally withdrawn, depressed or overweight.

This is where people find the benefits of the workshops. In these intimate groups, everyone is participating and working through their individual emotions, so they feel safe to share their experiences while encouraging each other along the way.

As you go through the process, remember, you have already been forgiven by the Creator. Isn't it time we extend grace to forgive ourselves as well as others?

> **"The LORD is compassionate and gracious, slow to anger, abounding in love. He does not treat us as our sins deserve or repay us according to our iniquities. as far as the east is from the west, so far has he removed our transgressions from us."**
>
> *- Psalms 103: 11-12*

Monday: Day 1 – First we're going to ask you to share the incident from your past with a friend, family member or even a counselor. Someone who feels safe enough to sit with you, hold you, cry with you if you need that. Someone who will support and encourage

you with words and actions that say I love you and I'm sorry this happened. Someone who will not only uplift you and walk with you through this difficult place but who will believe with you that you will overcome it. You may have to go outside your normal circle of friends to find that safe place.

Let them know that you're about to share something raw and vulnerable. Then share and allow that person to hold space for you by giving you nonjudgmental support and guidance. Maybe you don't need an answer, or instructions or a solution, maybe you just need someone to share your heart with and express your hurt. If that's the case, let them know that.

_____

_____

_____

_____

_____

Tuesday: Day 2 – Write down how you felt after sharing your story. What emotions came up for you? What were some of the uplifting and comforting words and thoughts you heard? What *Shifts* took place in your thinking during or after you shared your story?

_____

_____

_____

_____

_____

Wednesday: 3 – Today, ask The Spirit to show you if there is anyone that you need to say I'm sorry to or ask forgiveness of. Ask for the courage and the boldness to approach the person with humility and grace. After you've done so, write down how you felt. What emotions came up? What was *The Shift* you felt in your body, mind or emotions?

Remember, this is about you. About your healing process, so if things do not go as you expect, celebrate the fact that you're doing the work to release those negative emotions in order to receive your breakthrough. Don't be surprised if one of the people you have to apologize to is yourself.

_____

_____

_____

_____

_____

Thursday: Day 4 – For the rest of the week, as you feel led, seek out those individuals that came up for you that you need to forgive or say I'm sorry to. Then seek out ways to communicate with them. This may happen in a text, a phone call, over lunch or however you feel from the prompting of The Spirit.

_____

_____

_____

_____

_____

Friday: Day 5 – Spend the next three days in a place of gratefulness. Start by writing down all the things you are thankful for. Things as simple as "I woke up this morning" to "I have the use of my limbs. I have a roof over my head, a car that runs, children that are safe and food in my cabinets. I'm thankful for all the things my mother taught me before she left this earth."

Anything that comes up for you, write it down. Focusing on being thankful will shift the mindset from negative feelings to positive ones. Begin practicing this on a regular basis and you will begin to see *The Shift* you're desiring in your life.

_____

_____

_____

_____

_____

_____

Saturday: Reflection

Spend today meditating on the fact that you're being made new and things in your life are being restored. Find pleasure in knowing that, as you are releasing pent up emotions, you'll no longer have the need to feed them.

Celebrate that your mindset is changing as you continue to be in that place of thankfulness.

_____

_____

_____

_____

_____

Sunday: Be Still & Know –

Spend today just being still in a quiet place. In a park, on the beach, on a swing in your garden. Take time for yourself where you can be at peace. During this time, if there is anything you hear or see, write it below.

_____

_____

_____

_____

_____

Continue to incorporate the being and speaking what your grateful for, your mirror work, meditation, being physically active, eating fruits and vegetables, drinking 64 ounces of water, and doing your daily breathing as you embark on your journey to Oneness.

CHAPTER 8
"STUCK ON REPEAT" - WORDS OF AFFIRMATION

This must be a repeat.

I exhaled as I laid back into the sectional, crossing my legs at the ankles and burrowing my shoulders into the big pillows as if they were the arms of an old lover. Holding my breath, my eyes glued to the TV, I watched as the man's tall frame towered over hers. His bronze arms pulled her close as his head descended slowly towards hers. Quickly, I reached for the big bowl of tri-colored ice cream sitting in my lap. As the two actors exchanged a kiss, I shoveled a heaping tablespoon of creamy chocolate chip, butter pecan and pistachio-flavored ice cream into my mouth. Munching on the bits of deliciousness, I dug in for another, then another. I was riding the waves of a binge and my consumption was on autopilot.

Yup, I've been here before. This was definitely a repeat!

"Karen, are you aware of why you're eating?"

Above the slurping and lip-smacking, I heard that still small voice. I shook my head, trying to dislodge the thought and reached for the cold bottle of Coke next to the bag of Oreos on my coffee table. As I brought the bottle to my lips and took a huge gulp, I felt a stirring in the pit of my belly as the voice spoke again.

"Are you really hungry?"

"Oh no, pleeeaase," I put the bottle down and reached for the contents in the open bag of Doritos. "I know I asked for your help earlier," I reasoned, as I chewed on the chip, "but please, not now."

Watching the display of love on the tv, I ignored the voice as I took another swig of Coke, before popping the entire double stuff cream-filled Oreo in my mouth.

Having been through binges like this before, I knew if I just kept stuffing food in my mouth, the voice inside would eventually be quiet. So, I didn't slow down or stop to ponder the questions; I just kept eating, pausing only to wipe away the droplets of ice cream that fell on my shirt. I truly believed that if I focused on the spoon-to-bowl-to-mouth rotation, it would make the questions, thoughts and feelings go away.

But the questions always returned, especially after the binging. I wanted to ignore them. I believed if I concentrated more on what was in the bowl rather than the thoughts in my head, I wouldn't have to deal with the ache in my heart. The reality was, where my weekends were once filled with travel, dinners, dancing, musicals, movies, shows, amusement parks, etc., they were now replaced with this big empty couch, a table loaded with junk food, a dark, lonely living room and Hallmark movies. Hated it! Only I didn't know how to change it.

Although it brought some comfort initially, the excessive eating was certainly not helping, especially after finding that the 50 pounds I had lost two years earlier had returned with an additional 30 pounds to go with it. And the more I beat myself up with that fact, the more I ate. The high before the binge was always a thrill in the moment, but once I was left with only crumbs at the bottom of the bag, regret and shame quickly followed.

I was living in bondage to my past. Locked up in a jail cell with lies and negative thoughts. *Karen, you'll never get married. You're a terrible mother! Your son will never come back from college. In fact, he'll leave you just like his father did, and you'll probably end up eating yourself to death or dying of cancer like your mother.* My faith in the fear that life was always going to be an empty "dessert" container, broken promises and unfulfilled dreams was greater than my faith in the truth that I was a world-changer, born to conquer and create endless possibilities while living in abundance.

Rationally, I knew loss and change was the circle of life, but that did not diminish the fact that I felt abandoned, betrayed, alone, like someone lost at sea left to face the cold, dark and endless waters of shame, guilt and fear alone. I was on a roller coaster ride of emotions that I didn't want, or even know how to, get off of. So instead of facing them, I curled up in a fetal position in the corner of my existence and held on for dear life. I was too afraid to open my eyes and appreciate the opportunities, beauty and creation that life had to offer. I didn't want to share my struggle with anyone but food. Why? Because food never judged, talked back or gave an opinion. It simply comforted and it was always available.

Sitting on my couch weekend after weekend, binge-watching Netflix, isolating myself from life while devouring endless amounts of junk food was how I coped. I stuffed my feelings, so I didn't have to answer questions like *Why me? Why did he leave? Why did she die? Am I being too hard on my son? Will anyone ever love me? What happened? Why do I feel this way? What's wrong with me? What if ...? If only I would have...!* And the kicker—*How can I, a woman who feels so fragile, broken, beat down and depressed, raise this son of mine to be a bold, courageous, powerful, strong young man when I don't feel that way?*

I cried out to God and felt as hollow and empty as the bowl of ice cream I had just consumed. I was feeling deserted. Not only by my son's father, my mother, my family, but now feeling abandoned by God himself. Where was He? He could change these feelings, these emotions, my life, as easy as He changes the weather if he wanted, but instead He remained quiet. So, I did what any God-fearing woman who loved God would do. I checked out.

For six months, I did absolutely nothing but lie in bed and comfort myself with fast food, sugar-laden desserts and salty snacks of every kind while binge watching videos on YouTube of a dance duo called LesTwins. Their quick fluid movements mirrored every pulsating beat, tune, chord, strand of music they danced to; forming an expression of life. Their hands, arms legs became brushstrokes that painted the story they were telling through their musicality. Their movements were so interlaced with the music that it looked as if the sounds were being crafted by the moves they were making. For hours I would watch them, not knowing what it was about the brothers that captivated me. Perhaps it was their freedom to express, their power to create, their unbreakable connection. I wasn't sure, I can only tell you that they were my much-needed escape from the endless streams of negative thoughts that ran through my mind.

I was depressed! And I knew it, but I simply didn't care. I sat in that depression, no, *wallowed* in it. I let it cover me like a warm blanket, without fear and without judgment. And although I despised the oversized stop sign that seemed to be looming over my life in this season, I was at peace, believing that God was okay with me being right where I was and at some point, He was going to come for me.

Then one day, a friend from work who lived in my complex invited me over to meet a friend of hers who was visiting from out of town. And although I hated leaving the hug, I was receiving from my oversized pillows, feeling a pull from something outside myself, I went.

As soon as the pleasant introductions were made, I knew this was a God encounter. She had the same name as I did, only she was living the life I desired. Karen Robinson, founder of Solomon's Porch

Society was a strong, confident, married woman who traveled the world encouraging people to live their purpose. A coach, speaker, author and trainer, she was my mirror image, only on the other side of my current state of existence. Although petite in stature, this woman was bold, beautiful and a living, walking powerhouse! A hot air balloon whose colorful beauty and brilliance could be seen for miles. She took people on a journey out of their current place to rise up to see a bigger picture. She was confident, passionate and as fiery red as the blouse she wore; she looked me in my eyes and spoke to me about my gifts, the dreams I'd never voiced. Desires I didn't even know I had. Simply put, she said, "You are purpose with skin wrapped around it."

Hmmm, I thought, Now, what was I going to do about it?

We sat at the kitchen table, sipping tea, talking about our passions, her first, second and third book, and how she began walking in her calling. A soft glow from the light over the kitchen table fell over us. After much conversation, the light-heartedness of her voice changed to a serious tone that seemed to convey, *I need you to get this!*

"Karen, it's time to come out of hiding!" Uh oh, where had I heard that before?

"It's time to stop isolating yourself!" Who was this woman? She sounded like the small voice that often whispered to me during my binges.

"You were made to be at the forefront. It's where God has placed you. You have a desire to be on stage and in front of people because that's God's desire for you. He can trust you to be his mouthpiece!" My eyes began to fill with tears as I started to feel *a Shift* take place in my thinking. *God, is this true?*

She moved in closer, pinning me with her gaze, eyes locked on mine. She spoke with such conviction and so much assurance that I couldn't look away.

"Listen, there are many times where you began to take steps to walk in your purpose but recoiled back because people made you feel, or you yourself felt like you were acting more highly than you should, but you're not. That's God's heart for you."

I knew her words were coming from a higher place and I could feel each one penetrating my heart like the energizing jolt of a defibrillator. "God has given you a message that you need to share with the world. You were born to set the captives free. It's not just a feeling. It's your purpose. It's what you were born for." She continued, face now inches from mine. "Please come out. People are waiting for you; people need you. No more hiding. It's time to come out of isolation! It's time, Karen, it's time!"

I began to weep, head bowed, arms wrapped around my belly as if in pain, slowly rocking back and forth as waves of love and truth washed over me. She began to pray, and as she did, I could feel my spirit rise and stand at attention.

That night, God came for me!

Karen became my coach, and during our sessions, I could feel His Spirit ignite a new fire in me. Lies and crippling beliefs that were once shackles began to fall off, while hopes and dreams were birthed again.

Karen was just one of the many facets God used to cancel out the years of heartache, yo-yo dieting, emotional eating, depression and "mistaken" identity. By connecting my mind, body and spirit through transformational coaching, physical fitness and spiritual healing, *The Shift* took place. I was able to overcome fear and walk in my God-given identity.

Although I had been practicing transformational coaching and speaking work for years under the guise of spiritual counseling and youth leadership, I officially launched KNX Journey to Oneness in May 2018.

I not only live out that vision God gave me in 2004 that you read about in the Introduction of this book, I'm also a published author, transformational coach, speaker and health and wellness trainer, walking in my purpose and living my dreams. My mind, body and soul have been set free. I've released more than 80 pounds and no longer allow emotional eating or negative thinking to control my life. I'm not saying life is perfect, but I can say I'm living and loving life. My calling is to help others find their true identity, find their purpose, and live their best life.

Are you ready to begin living yours?

WEEK 8 ACTIVITY
SPEAKING WORDS OF AFFIRMATION

This week we're going to focus on speaking words of affirmation.

We're going to affirm ourselves by speaking words of love and encouragement that will begin to change our thinking.

To affirm is to give yourself (life) a heightened sense of value, typically through the experience of something emotionally or spiritually uplifting. The act of declaring affirmation over oneself is to offer yourself emotional support or encouragement.

As you can see from this chapter, I was telling myself false truths like, "You will never get married." "You're a terrible Mother. Nobody wants you." These negative thoughts and lies were keeping me in a place of bondage.

"What a man thinks in his heart, so he is."
- Proverbs 23:7

Because I thought that way, I lived this way—in scarcity, brokenness, unforgiveness doubt and fear.

But The Spirit tells us to.

"Fix your thoughts on what is true, and honorable, and right, and pure, and lovely, and admirable. Think about things that are excellent and worthy of praise."
- Philippians 4:8

Imagine yourself speaking to a loved one or a child. When the child makes a mistake or does something wrong, the hope as you admonish them is to speak words with love, correction and encouragement with the intent to change their behavior. Words like, "Try again! Don't give up! You can do it! I believe in you!"

> **"Therefore, as God's chosen people, holy and dearly loved, clothe yourselves with compassion, kindness, humility, gentleness and patience."**
>
> *- Colossians 3:12*

If we've been given this charge to treat others this way, why wouldn't we give ourselves the same treatment?

This week we're going to put on the shirt of compassion, the slacks of kindness, and the shoes of patience. We will speak words out loud to ourselves that will change our minds, fill our hearts, and help us to begin to love ourselves.

For an example of the activity we will be doing this week, go to my website, www.KNXone.com, and click on the tab "Words of Affirmation" under the page labeled "The Shift."

Start this week with:

- Breathing 4-5 minutes

- Answer the three questions below.

- Each day spend a few minutes in prayer and meditation asking The Spirit to share words that speak to your identity.

- Write down the words you hear, then spend each day speaking those words out loud to yourself. If you find yourself speaking or saying negative things to yourself, STOP! Take that thought captive, apologize to yourself, and ask God to share words with you that speak to your identity. Speak His words to your emotions. Do this every day of the week as the activity states.

Ask The Spirit to show you what lies you've been believing. (i.e. "I'll never get married; I'm the worst performer at my job; I'll never be able to afford a home," etc.)

_____

_____

_____

_____

_____

Ask God to show you a truth to counter that lie.

_____

_____

_____

_____

_____

Write down that truth, put it up where you can see it, and speak it out loud to yourself every morning.

_____

_____

_____

_____

_____

Monday: Spend each day speaking words of affirmation out loud to yourself. If you find yourself speaking or thinking negative things about yourself, STOP! Take that thought captive,

apologize, and ask God to share words with you that speak to your identity, not your emotions. Do this every day of the week.

_____

_____

_____

_____

Tuesday:

_____

_____

_____

_____

Wednesday:

_____

_____

_____

_____

Thursday:

_____

_____

_____

_____

Friday:

_____

_____

_____

_____

_____

Saturday: Replenish: Spend time being thankful for all the words of affirmation you heard this week.

_____

_____

_____

_____

_____

Sunday: Be Still & Know –

Spend today just being still in a quiet place. In a park, on the beach, on a swing in your garden. Take time for yourself where you can be at peace. During this time, if there is anything you hear or see, write it below.

_____

_____

_____

_____

_____

Continue to incorporate the daily practice of speaking words of affirmation, being thankful, your mirror work, meditation, being physically active, eating fruits and vegetables, drinking 64 ounces of water, and doing your daily breathing as you embark on your journey to Oneness.

CHAPTER 9
THE NIGHT THE SPIRIT SPOKE - VISUALIZATION

If you're like me, you know what it feels like to put yourself on a strict diet, lose those unwanted pounds, only to find them again several months later plus more! Why? Well, there's often something deep within us that we're battling, some type of trauma that is keeping us bound, something we have yet to truly deal with or overcome! A divorce, loss of a job, death of a loved one, a rebellious child, etc. Because of this unchecked pain, we use methods of numbing, like emotional eating, isolation, and addictive behaviors to shut up the lies we're believing and the negative thinking we fill our heads with.

The struggle with emotional eating caused me to embark on numerous diets, like Weight Watchers, Jenny Craig, The Atkins Diet, low carb, to name a few. In addition, I would spend hours in the gym running, squatting, lifting, benching and yes, I would eventually see the weight come off. However, while I was focused on my outer appearance, I was not seeking healing for the emotional turmoil that was going on within me. I used food as a device to deal with the internal trauma that went unchecked. I was trying to put a band-aid on an open gash. So, it wasn't long before the "wound" would get infected, the emotions would take over, the mindless eating would begin again, and the weight would return.

God began to reveal to me that my war with food did not start at the refrigerator, the convenience store, the fast-food joint, or on the plate I hovered over; it started in my mind.

What I fixed my eyes on!

What I allowed to enter my ears.

What I replayed in my mind or said to myself.

These were the driving factors that made me run to food as a source of peace, comfort or release. As I learned this, I finally started seeking tools that went beyond salads, water and hours at the gym.

I introduced the practice of visualization into my healing process after listening to Geneen Roth's audiobook, *When Food is Food and Love is Love.* The title of her book is what initially caught my attention, but after reading the first few pages, I was captivated. Geneen was speaking directly to where I was in my life.

In this chapter, you will find the story of my first visualization process, where God brought healing around the negative belief that my life would be cut short like my mother's. This practice was instrumental in bringing truth to the lies I was believing.

We believe you too will receive breakthrough using this practice. As you can see from the verse below, visualization relates back to God's plan for you.

"Then the Lord answered me and said: "Write the vision and make it plain on tablets, that he may run who reads it."
- Habakkuk 2:2

THE VISUALIZATION:

The vines, long, thick and full of deep olive colored leaves, slowly swayed as if dancing to the soft breeze that blew around me. Trees, with endless branches painted in green, embraced me on every side as I looked at the vastness of God's creation. In the cool of the morning, I could see the glimmer of sunlight peeking through the lush forest as the tree branches hung low enough to brush my head and drape my shoulders. As I slowly made my way through the vines, bending down under some and pushing others aside, I felt empty of any worries or concerns, yet full to the brim with anticipation and excitement bubbling up in me at what was to come.

Like a theater curtain being drawn, the forest suddenly opened wide, making a clearing! In a flash, there she was, bathed in a stream of light that showed off her mahogany brown skin and matching eyes. Her smile, wide on either side of her cheeks, displayed that beautiful dimple I loved so much. I stopped, unaware that I was holding my breath. Was I really seeing who I thought I was seeing?

"Mom?" With that simple thought she was instantly standing before me, no longer space between us. No longer death between us. Her gaze shifted with delight as her wide brown eyes surveyed mine. Her mouth was slightly open in wonder and disbelief as she searched my face, looking deep within. No words were exchanged, although I could hear everything she was saying. All that she was feeling. I was feeling the same.

Suddenly, she lifted her shoulders, straightened her back and raised her neck, standing tall and upright; I mirrored her stance. I knew what she was saying although she wasn't using words. "Walk in strength. Walk with dignity. Walk in power, my daughter." Knowing that I had gotten her message, her smile widened, showing her beautiful white teeth and a sparkle that reached her eyes.

Taking my face in her hands, I could feel her warmth as she cupped either side of my cheeks; I felt her love and how proud she was of me. I put my hands on hers and like the display of creation around us, I could see her beauty and vibrancy. The joy exuding from her bubbled over and embraced me. She was full of life and love and I could feel it. She was pleased with who I had become.

Suddenly, I sensed something black and sinister enter the core of her. As we stood there it began to consume her, I felt as if it was becoming harder to hold onto her. I could no longer feel the warmth of her hands on my face or the softness of her skin. As the blackness grew, it seemed to overtake her. She was no longer there with me. The vision of her smile, the strength of her stance, her gentle touch, her very existence, was gone and I couldn't sense or feel her anymore. Her beauty and her radiance were no longer present. Like a vapor of smoke, she seemed to have dissipated into thin air. Even the colors of nature that surrounded us faded and became like ash.

As I came out of the visualization exercise, I was shaken and confused.

"God, what do you want to say to me about this?"

"Karen, you do not have cancer. You are not going to die from cancer. All that you are and all that you desire to be is in Me, is Me. I am the truth, the life, and the way. Everything else is a lie. I came to give life and to give it more abundantly."

"Then how come she didn't have abundant life?"

"I'm sorry Karen; her death grieved me as it grieved you. But you are not your mother. That cancer, that blackness, will not consume you. You are not your mother. You are not your mother. The plans I have for you are to give you a hope and a future. It is not to harm you. I love you. Trust Me!"

"Lord, please teach me how. With everything in me I'm trying. Please teach me how."

"I AM."

As you prepare yourself for this week's activity, believe that God is continuing to do a transformation in you. The Spirit brought healing to me through the practice of visualization; I believe God will bring healing to you as well. If you feel this week becomes too overwhelming in any way, please consult your regular physician or medical counselor for professional advice or counseling.

For example and information on the activity you will be doing this week, go to my website at www.KNXone.com and click on the tab "Visualization Exercise" under the page labeled "The Shift!"

WEEK 9 ACTIVITY
CAN YOU SEE IT? - VISUALIZATION

This week's exercise is to spend time participating in the following Visualization Exercises:

- Pick one of the three visualization exercises to do each morning, evening or when time permits.

- Find a quiet, secluded place where you will have no interruptions or distractions.

- Set aside at least 10-20 minutes for the exercise. Increase your time as you get more familiar with the practice. Remember, The Spirit desires to speak to you more than you desire to hear.

- Incorporate your breathing exercises until you find yourself centered and at peace.

- Try selecting a different exercise from the three below each day so you have an opportunity to practice each one. However, if you feel The Spirit bringing you back to the same exercise or vision, go with it! More may be revealed to you during each session or throughout the day or even weeks.

- After each visualization practice, journal about what you hear, see, and feel during your time.

Start by answering the three questions below.

What kinds of feelings are you experiencing in your body?

_____

_____

_____

_____

What thoughts are going through your mind?

_____

_____

_____

_____

How are you feeling from a spiritual perspective?

_____

_____

_____

_____

After answering the three questions above, sit still and ask The Spirit to bring you a picture, feeling, idea or thought that He wants to speak with you about. Then wait. As He begins to share with you the revelation, begin asking what's being shown to you and why. Then wait for a response.

Stay in the moment—don't rush the process and don't be discouraged if you don't hear or see something immediately. This is a practice like anything else and it may take time before you hear clearly.

Visualize yourself in the future where you would like to be. In that new job, starting that business, going back to school, landing that contract, living in that home, in that relationship, spending time with those children. Make a note of whatever you see.

Take a scripture, a word, a promise, or a picture that you feel The Spirit has given you. As you begin to see it in your mind, visualize it coming to pass. Ask God to give you specific details.

Each day, on the space provided, make a note of what you heard, saw, and felt after your visualization exercise.

Monday:

_____

_____

_____

_____

Tuesday:

_____

_____

_____

_____

Wednesday:

_____

_____

_____

_____

Thursday:

_____

_____

_____

_____

Friday:

_____

_____

_____

_____

Saturday: Reflection

Spend today meditating on things God has spoken to you this week. Write down what you see, hear or feel.

_____

_____

_____

_____

Sunday: Be Still & Know –

Spend today just being still in a quiet place. In a park, on the beach, on a swing in your garden. Take time for yourself where you can be at peace. During this time, if there is anything you hear or see, write it below.

_____

_____

_____

_____

Continue to incorporate the daily exercise of visualization, being grateful, your mirror work, meditation, being physically active, eating fruits and vegetables, drinking 64 ounces of water, and doing your daily breathing as you embark on your journey to Oneness.

Remember this is a process. A journey that you will continue to walk out daily. At any point if you need to revisit a chapter, or go through the book again, please do so. It's not a magic formula or instant fix. It's a daily practice of walking with The Spirit of God and allowing His Spirit to lead you into your place of freedom. Step by step. Day by day.

If you feel like you could use additional support, accountability or coaching after completing The Shift, you may want to consider signing up for a KNX Journey to Oneness workshop or 1-1 coaching with Karen. Find out how in the next chapter.

Congratulations! You have completed The Shift - Your Journey to Breakthrough

CHAPTER 10
WHAT IS KNX JOURNEY TO ONENESS AND HOW DO I SIGN UP FOR A

WORKSHOP or PERSONAL COACHING?

KNX Journey to Oneness Workshops are based on the book *The Shift*

Our minds produce about 50,000 to 70,000 thoughts a day. Whether we realize it or not, these thoughts have an effect on our bodies, health, and emotions. What we're thinking can either keep us motivated and uplifted, or feeling hopeless and bound. That's where KNX Journey to Oneness comes into play.

In the KNX Journey to Oneness Workshops, we focus on connecting the Mind, Body, and The Spirit by using mechanisms that will bring healing and restoration.

Declarations and affirmations will be used to eradicate false beliefs, while truth and negative self-talk will be eliminated, resulting in *The Shift* of thinking and a new belief and love for oneself.

Physical activity, healthy nutrition, rest and self-care will help fuel your body, boost your mood, shed unwanted pounds as well as tone and shape your butt, hips and thighs.

Spirit-led coaching using meditation, deep breathing and visualization will evoke your inner voice to hear and envision answers within that will guide you into freedom, abundance and purpose.

The Biggest Benefit of the Workshops is it provides personal interaction. Based on my book *The Shift*, I have created live and virtual workshops that focus on deeper healing and transformation, either one-on-one or in a group setting.

During these 9-week workshops, we will go in-depth with each of the chapters outlined in the book, but we'll also practice self-love and self-care for our bodies and minds. By using other modalities like physical fitness, nutrition and the word of God. We will replace negative thoughts with the truth of who God says we are, resulting in a lifestyle of freedom and breakthrough.

KNX Journey to Oneness's purpose is not to promote one diet over another. The mission is to educate people on how to choose the healthiest foods for the body in order to live in optimal wellness.

In the Workshops, you will experience hands-on training in:

- Learning How to Make Fresh Juice and the Benefits of Juicing

- Performing a Cleansing Detoxification

- The Benefits of Eating a Clean Diet

- Discovering What is "Processed Food" vs. "Living Foods"

- Chemicals and Toxins in the Body

- Why We Should Incorporate a Plant-Based Diet

- What to Eat to Decrease Your Chances (or Even Reverse) Ailments Such as Cardiovascular Disease, Diabetes, Arthritis, Depression, Inflammation, etc.

- How to Use the Bible to Eradicate Negative Thinking

- Meal Prepping and So Much More

- Participate in an Exercise Workout (Optional)

Results:

As people learn about mindfulness, nutrition and exercise, they begin to see their bodies as the temple God designed it to be. They choose to move their bodies, eat food for fuel rather than comfort, and incorporate self-care and self-love.

> **"After all, no one ever hated their own body, but they feed and care for their body, just as Christ does the church."**
>
> *- Ephesians 5:29*

Here's what people are saying about KNX Workshops, Coaching and Retreats:

I had the pleasure to FINALLY experience Karen's services at my signature 'Still I Rise' retreat in San Diego. It was a REFRESHING experience to begin our day with a SUNRISE workout by the water. Karen is relatable; she is a testament via her appearance alone of what SELF LOVE and the pursuit of SELF RESTORATION looks like! She moves beyond the theory of a great story to a living, walking, talking, put in the work testimony of SELF. It was an EXPERIENCE of FULL BODY & MIND ENGAGEMENT! A divinely welcomed experience... – Veronica Simon

First, Karen truly loves and cares about her clients and that is so important to me. She realizes not everyone is at the same level and having modifications is very important. I also had the pleasure of experiencing one of her meditation sessions and it was "just what I needed." She helped me focus on the positive and taught me to "let go." Her enthusiasm, energy and spirit are so comforting! I recommend giving Karen a try...she won't disappoint! – Cindy Spillar

A well spent 6-week investment for myself. I'm still unpacking all the reflection and knowledge nuggets I picked up along the way. Karen allowed herself to be the vessel used to help guide me to peel back layers of emotional baggage that was hindering my growth. I wanted to grow, and I wanted more connection with my husband and friends, and I was unsure how to move forward. I found myself stuck and frustrated on an ongoing basis. Working with Karen allowed me to reflect and pray and cry and find joy again. Thank you, Karen, for your patience and love! Thank you for your obedience. – Angela Ching

If you are ready to sign up for a live or virtual workshop, or would just like more information, go to www.KNXone.com and click on the tab under "Programs."

Workshops/Retreats

Personal 1–1 Training

Group Fitness

Speaking Engagements

Beautiful

by Carolyn Mitchell

I was scrolling through recent Facebook posts and came across this picture with a woman posing while lying on the ground; in big bold white letters painted on the ground was the word "BEAUTIFUL."

At first glance you say, "That's a cute picture," then hit the infamous "like" button, as many others did. I'm pretty sure they were captivated by the "beauty" of the picture as well as the "Beauty" in the picture. So, I left the comment, "What a beauty!"

After posting that remark, I looked again at the picture and Karen in the picture. Only this time, my eyes zoomed in on what would be the obvious: Karen's physical image had changed. I've heard from her in times past that her physical image had changed numerous times, some good, but mostly bad. However, this time the physical change of her outward appearance had devastated her, and she seemed to have lost hope. So, I looked again at Karen lying on the ground specifically her face.

Wow!

I was blown away by Karen's face! What a glow she carried upon her. I looked at her radiant smile and saw the light of Love, and I said to myself again, "Wow!" I totally agreed with her about the outward physical change, but I looked at her and saw a NEW woman!

Karen has missed the greatest change about her, and it had nothing to do with the outward appearance but everything to do with the internal change.

I saw a woman grounded in her beautiful Father!

I saw a woman purified by her beautiful Father!

I saw a woman resting confidently in her beautiful Father's arms!

I saw the light of her beautiful Father surrounding her!

I saw a woman who had changed and been released from the former woman she was, but now clothed with real "beauty"!

So, I say to you, Karen, it doesn't matter what ups and downs you encounter with the outward appearance; what matters is the continual pursuit of allowing your beautiful Father to enhance the "beauty" on the inside of you. Accept who you are today, Karen!

Don't get angry with it, don't run from it, don't dwell on your past about what you used to look like. Don't hide anymore! Come face to face with your "beauty" and accept where you are. Once you accept where you are, you will move past the disappointment and release the false sense of security you have been living with.

Release the control to your beautiful Father; His hands are open to receive you Karen. Your new life is "Now!" It's not contingent upon getting back to the perfect body image. It's "Now"!

"No one lights a lamp and then puts it under a basket. Instead, a lamp is placed on a stand, where it gives light to everyone in the house."

- *Matthew 5:15*

I love you, "Beautiful!"

Overcomer

by Jesse Boykins

Overcome by sin in my darkest hour
I call on your name
The one who conquered the grave on Calvary
One died but millions were saved
Blessed is the Name
That is the Name that makes the devil tremble
And saved and blessed is every son
and daughter who is resting in green meadows
And lead by still waters
Your rod and your staff comfort me
How can this be, I was blind and now I see
Touched by the Presence of the most-high King
Did not sit with kings but sat with peasants
My God is miraculous, He gives me strength
So now I overcome sin because
His light shines in my darkest hour

And You Shall Be Called by A New Name –

OVERCOMER!

photo credit: Linda Krellner Photography

Wellness Physical Activity Readiness (PAR-Q) Questionnaire

Health and Wellness is a process that involves more than just exercise! Please take the time to answer these questions, so that you can better tailor a health and wellness program to suit your specific needs.

Name:_____ Date:_____

Gender:_____Height:_____Weight:_____Age & Date of Birth_____

Measurements: Bust_____Waist_____Thighs _____Hips_____Stomach

Yes	No	
Yes	No	Has a physician ever said you have a heart condition and you should only perform physical activity recommendations by a physician?
Yes	No	When you perform physical activity, do you feel pain in your chest.
Yes	No	Have you had chest pain, while not performing physical activity, in the past month?
Yes	No	Do you ever lose consciousness, or do you lose your balance because of dizziness?
Yes	No	Do you suffer from any major muscle or joint conditions that may limit you or be aggravated by physical activity?
Yes	No	Do you suffer from any medical conditions that may be made worse by participating in physical activity?
Yes	No	Is a physician currently prescribing medications for any of the following blood pressure, heart condition, asthma, diabetes, etc.
Yes	No	Do you suffer from high blood pressure over 140/90 or low blood pressure below 100/80?
Yes	No	Are you pregnant?
Yes	No	Do you have insulin-dependent diabetes?
Yes	No	Are you 69 years of age or older?
Yes	No	Do you know of any other reason you should not exercise or increase your physical activity?

Disclaimer:
If you have answered no to all of the above questions and you are confident that you have no other concerns with your health then you may proceed to participate in physical activity. If you have answered yes to any of the questions above or are unsure, please seek a referral from your GP or allied health professional before commencing physical activity.

I believe to the best of my knowledge that all of the information I have provided on this tool is accurate. In the case that my medical condition changes over the course of my training I will inform my trainer and fill out a new exercise pre-screening questionnaire.

Client signature:_____Trainer signature: _____Date:_____

THANK YOU

Gordon and Gloria Nurse – I am who I am today because of you! Thank you for your love, strength and determination and all that you instilled in me. I hope I make you proud. I love you!

The Nurse Family – I love you! I pray this book will bring peace and encouragement to you in some way. Thank you for your love and support.

David and Erin Nurse – The words "You should be a writer" gave me the freedom and courage to write this book. Being a single mother, you are the family we so desperately needed! Thank you for always believing in us, supporting us and for being there for us! Thank you for choosing us even when it was ugly and scary. Thank you for being true examples of Christ! We love you!

Carolyn Mitchell and Angela Boykins – Where would I be without you? You have seen me and walked my son and I through every stage of this book. You probably could tell this story for me. Thank you for being my dearest friends. My sisters! My family! Thank you that even in my fear, my isolation, my depression, my hurt, anger and pain, you never turned your back on us. Though we've grown, evolved, separated through time and space, we've remained friends, and I'm so grateful. Thank you for praying me through the storm and standing with me today in His glory. There are not enough words to tell you what you mean to me. So grateful that we get to and will continue to do life together! My love for you abounds!

My Loves Keilan, Kyree, Jesse –Thank you for always being present. Thank you for never complaining about the late nights, for always being in church, for the prayer vigils that went into the wee hours of the morning. For letting us drag you wherever we thought Jesus would be. I love you! Thank you for being our family.

Angela Ching – An example of true love, obedience and surrender to the Father. Truly my inspiration. I am so utterly grateful for you. Thank you for hearing and receiving my heart even at times when I didn't know what it was saying. Thank you for believing that there is more to "abundance" than what we've been believing. Thank you for believing in me and my son and for speaking life into KNX. Thank you for always pointing me back to the Father. I love you! Yours is next!

Alexis Asbe – I am hopelessly and forever devoted to you, my Queen. Thank you for pursuing and wooing me out of my darkest place and walking with me into His marvelous light. Thank you for seeing me when I couldn't see myself. Thank you for challenging me to go beyond my fear and step into the bravest, deepest most intimate relationship I could be in. The one with myself. Thank you for loving me without judgement or criticism. I am who I am today because of your faith in me. Thank you for being my strategic coach, my visionary, my push that helped me to get past my fear. I am a published author and coach because of you! My love for you is bottomless!

Chrysalis Group – Thank you for accepting me and embracing me when you barely knew me. Thank you for allowing me to be naked and vulnerable before you while you spun your casing of love around me so I could become the butterfly I am today. Angele Overstreet, Lori Wiggan, Anjuli Belle Crouch. I love you! Carrie Grosch, I remember our talks and prayers about being in this place of freedom one day. Thank you for not only being a safe and loving place of peace and wisdom to me but to my son as well! I love you, my friend!

My Brothers and Sisters at CBN – "Some men came carrying a paralyzed man on a sleeping mat. They tried to take him inside to Jesus, but they couldn't reach him because of the crowd. So, they went up to the roof and took off some tiles. Then they lowered the sick man on his mat down into the crowd, right in front of Jesus. Seeing their faith, Jesus said to the man, 'Friend, your sins are forgiven.'" *Luke 5:18-20* - Thank you for your love, your words and your prayers. Nathan Jan, Peyman Jan, Mikey, Tyler, Bettina, Edwin Jan, Mike A., Daniel, Chris. They carried me to Him.

Aaron, Jeremiah and Matthew – Thank you for being the men my son needed to see. I love you!

Carlos and Katherine Miras – The way you love us is truly a gift! Your words and ways changed our lives! There's no way I could repay you. Your friendship means everything. Thank you! I love you!

My Editors, Designers, Photographers and Publishers, etc. – I am so grateful! For the edits, the photos, the website, the suggestions, the advice, the praise, etc. - however you played a part in the production of this book, I'm truly grateful. Thank you!

To the Ladies of View 202 – You know who you are! Thank you for seeing who I was then! The women of Esther! I love you!

My Prayer Warriors – You know who you are. The ones that get the 3:00 am text that says, "Can you please pray for…" Thank you for always saying Yes! For standing in the gap so the King can hear and respond. So absolutely grateful for each of you!

To everyone who has been a part of my life who is not mentioned by name - Thank you. This book is dedicated to you as well! Thank you for the love, prayers, encouragement, support and contributions recently and over the years. For both my son and I. For all that you've been and done in our lives, we thank you.

ASL – Thank you for the gift of our son. I am an Overcomer and We have been redeemed.

5/30/2020

Karen Nurse

Dear Pastor Sandy!

How are you. I pray this find you well. Thank you so much for investing your love and book. Truly appreciate your love and support. Immediately in my spirit I feel like I'm hearing the words stand tall. Although the Tide is High you firmly PLANTED and I feel like I looked up Tide on Google and the Tide is High song by Blondie is for you now. The Tide is High But I'm Holding on. I'm Gonna be your number 1. Might be good to look up the words. When an apple I shaken its only the fruit that has happened is not in vain. All that is grown ripe and delicious. That fruit is then given to feed others but more seeds will also be for those who eat the fruit who in turn will produce more fruit. Not yet come but when it come it could produce a harvest that's a 100 fold. Be still and know. I AM GOD also in your waiting, waiting know THIS TOO SHALL PASS. GOD HAS A MULTITUDE of BLESSINGS with your name on it. May this book richly bless you my friend I will